CHASING THE ELEPHANT INTO THE BUSH

THE POLITCS OF COMPLACENCY

Arthur Kennedy

authorHOUSE®

AuthorHouse™
1663 Liberty Drive
Bloomington, IN 47403
www.authorhouse.com
Phone: 1-800-839-8640

First published by AuthorHouse 10/26/2009

ISBN: 978-1-4490-3705-5 (e)
ISBN: 978-1-4490-3703-1 (sc)
ISBN: 978-1-4490-3704-8 (hc)

Library of Congress Control Number: 2009910731

Printed in the United States of America
Bloomington, Indiana

This book is printed on acid-free paper.

ACKNOWLEDGEMENTS

THANKING PEOPLE IS A PLEASANT BUT risky exercise. There is always the possibility that someone who deserves thanks may be overlooked.

Let me begin by thanking my wife, Nana Ama, and my sons, Kwamina and Kofi, for their patience and support as I went through one of the most exciting periods in my life. I could not have done this without them.

Next, I thank the teachers in my life, for all that they have taught me. As some of the experiences recounted in this book show, I have not always been easy to teach or direct. Of these teachers, none has touched my life more than the two Medical doctors, Dr. A.B.A. Prempeh of the Ghana Medical School and Dr. Osei Asibey, a member of Parliament in the Third Republic. Dr Prempeh encouraged me to contest for the Presidency of the National Union of Ghana Students, NUGS, in 1983 at a very difficult time in Ghana's history and pledged his support when needed and he has been better than his word, through my many ups and downs. I cannot say enough about how significant he has been to my political life.

I spent a year living with Dr. Osei Asibey in Grande-Bassam, in the Ivory Coast before proceeding to America in 1988. Every evening, after work, he would recount his experiences during the Limann administration and point out where they went wrong and how things could have been done better as I listened attentively. My third teacher was Professor John McCracken of the University of Texas at Dallas, my main teacher for my Masters Program in Medical Management. He showed me how to apply the tools of Medical Diagnoses and post-mortems to management and leadership. As I watched events unfold in the campaign, I could imagine my class putting these events under the microscope and Dr. McCracken asking repeatedly "But why did you do that?" This is an attempt to apply some of the skills I acquired to our campaign that was about leadership, change and communication.

I owe a lot to those who gave so much of their time, their intellect and their money to my campaign.

Despite all these, without the 2008 NPP Presidential Candidate, Nana Akufo-Addo, putting me on his team and giving me such a valuable perch from which to participate and to observe the campaign, this book would not be possible. I thank him. Many in the campaign, particularly Jake Obetsebi-Lamptey and Dr. Owusu Afriyie Akoto, were very kind in helping me adapt to the campaign environment. Prof. Larry Gibson taught me a lot about polls and their significance in politics.

While I was locked into debate with myself as to whether to write this book or not, I met uncle Ebo White of "Frustrated wives-Confused husbands" fame, whom I had known at Legon. When he asked whether I would write a book, I cited cost as an obstacle. To my amazement, he said "If you write such a book and need help publishing it, let me know." The next day, I started writing.

Many have helped me with this book. They include political analyst, Mr. Ben Ephson and Mr. Antwi Agyei, the NPP administrator, who made many useful suggestions and filled me in on historical details. These two gentlemen have an inexhaustible fund of stories and they kept me off schedule with great political stories.

Finally, I thank Mr. Boadu Ayeboafoh, the 1995 GJA Journalist of the year, who took time off his vacation to write the foreword and Mr. Bismarck Badu, the ever-present force who kept prodding everyone to keep moving.

Despite all these contributions, the errors are mine.

Arthur Kobina Kennedy

FOREWORD

ELECTIONS ARE FUNDAMENTAL AND CRUCIAL TO the sustainability and stability of democratic governance. It is therefore more than imperative that everything is done to safeguard and give meaning to the franchise and with that the choice of the people.

In 1992, following allegations of fraud and irregularities in the November 7th presidential election, the New Patriotic Party (NPP) led a boycott of the parliamentary polls that year, resulting in a near one-party Parliament. The party equally published "The Stolen Verdict", which chronicled the irregularities the party noted during the election.

Having then accused the ruling government of rigging, the NPP as a government, had the responsibilities to ensure the December 2008 general elections was not only free and fair but peaceful and orderly. It is, therefore, heart-warming that the author decided to put his observations and developments during the process into perspective. What is important is that he was a participant in most of the issues and events he has chronicled, while in some others he was either an active or passive observer. The beauty of the work is that an attempt has been made from within to permanently preserve the factors that combined to affect the fortunes of the NPP.

It is always better for people to tell their own stories. If they fail to do so, others will tell the story for them. But when you tell your own story, the approach is different from when an outsider does that and purports to know and understand matters better than the participants themselves. For the first time in the history of the NPP, the author has brought up crucial internal matters, some of which could have been glossed over and taken for granted, but which have serious consequences for the future of the party.

The author, being Communications Director of the NPP campaign and before that an aspirant himself, had insight into events and issues as they unfolded. Although actively involved, he does not surrender to, but is able to objectively chronicle issues for the public and the party hierarchy. He equally manages to confirm some of the rumours which made the rounds about the abuse of money "moneycracy" in our politics and admits that he too parted with money at some point in the process. He also tackled the "Kyebi Mafia" and addressed it in such a measured and temperate manner that it does not cause offense, the way it was made to look by those who were far from the process of the electioneering campaign by Nana Addo Dankwa Akufo-Addo. For instance, on the so-called Mafia, he writes that "it is very impressive that Nana Akufo-Addo has a large family and associates who are all eager to help him realize his political ambitions. They should be commended for their interest in him and in politics…"

"I have no doubt that the family has the best intentions in whatever they do. However, sometimes, in their eagerness to serve Nana's interest, they ruffle feathers, sometimes very badly and gratuitously."

These are candid views which a person who wishes the other to progress would point out. For as it has been observed, "the best compliment that one can make to a friend is to be candid with him." That is food for thought for the future.

Another area worth noting is the observation that it appeared that most often, the local politicians with whom the voters identified were not allowed to address them at the local rally, giving way to self-serving individuals who spoke to enhance their egos, rather than to help the cause of the party and the candidate. It is equally important that those who blamed certain individuals for the failure of the party to win power, on reading this book, will appreciate how these persons sacrificed for the cause of the party, especially the role of former President John Agyekum Kufuor. The admission that the party shot itself in the leg, particularly in the inability of layers of leadership to reconcile their differences, is interesting. So is the revelation that the spending committee's activities remained a mystery, as individuals maneuvered to get funding while activities of the accredited committees were denied financial resources. Another interesting development is the issue of the report of the consultant, Larry Gibson, which indicated that the National Democratic Congress could win the polls, and how and why the party failed to heed some of his recommendations on the nature and procedure for campaigning.

Yet another insight is how Nana Akufo-Addo was denied the privilege of choosing the running mate he preferred, but had to settle for somebody who was never in the equation and did not appear ready at the time he was named.

Arthur Kennedy has done something functional for the party and members should read the book with keen interest and readiness to learn from it so that "if we put our house in order, pick good parliamentary candidates, get our people to vote, get our votes counted so that we have each of the twenty-two thousand (22,000) polling station results signed and verified on election day of 2012, nobody can steal it from us."

Whether the book will prick our conscience and enable us to act appropriately, time will tell. But to those who will read the book, Arthur Kennedy does not leave anyone in doubt that if the party takes note of its weaknesses and strengths as recounted , they will see to recapturing of political power in 2012.

- YAW BOADU-AYEBOAFOH, 1995 JOURNALIST OF THE YEAR, GHANA JOURNALISTS ASSOCIATION.

24TH JUNE, 2009.

ACCRA, GHANA

TABLE OF CONTENTS

INTRODUCTION

"To see and not to speak will be the great betrayal"

Enoch Powell, American Conservative in 1968

Since the 2008 elections, I have been asked repeatedly for my views on why the New Patriotic Party (NPP) lost the general elections.

Surprisingly, these requests have not only come from members of the public. They have also come from NPP members, some of whom I respect very much.

I have decided to write for three reasons.

First, sometime ago, when I responded to one such request by invoking the cost, the response I received surprised me. The person who had made the request promised to help get the book published if I would write it. Second, some friends have been reminding me of my frequent complaints that there is a dearth of respectable literature and references from practicing politicians on politics in Ghana.

The final reason is that , it will begin the effort of setting the record straight. There are too many people out there with good intentions and little information about what happened who are out there, in the media, on the internet and at funerals and parties working hard to fill the vacuum with information or to be more accurate, misinformation.

While this book may not compare with the high standards of academic literature written elsewhere, I hope it will encourage more people with first-hand experience to write. In the past, I asked seasoned politicians, including William Ofori-Atta AKA Paa Wille and Victor Owusu to write but they did not. Now, I wish I could read books written by people like P.V. Obeng, Kojo Mpiani and Sam Okudzeto, to mention a few. This is a small attempt to practice what I preach.

To get to the answers about why the NPP lost, we need to know what happened. There are some, including at the highest levels of our campaign who believe that the only thing that went wrong was our failure to police the vote on Election Day. While our failure on voting day was most significant, I believe it is the most glaring manifestation of the systemic failures that together caused our defeat. I believe that by the beginning of 2007, the NPP had enough support to win a Presidential election with 54% or more and to increase our Parliamentary seats by five to ten. However, we proceeded to make mistakes, in government, in our party and in campaigning that by election-day, had us with a narrow but significant lead. Going into election-day, the only issue was whether the NPP would win one-touch or need a second round. Then on election-day, we failed to protect that vote.

This book is an attempt to re-create the campaign as I saw it. Therefore it will be limited in its scope. While I will cover events as broadly and as fairly as possible, I was not in every meeting and cannot recount everything with a completely balanced perspective. An effort like this is the equivalent of a group of blind people describing an elephant. Each one touches a different part of the elephant and therefore describes it, differently. During the campaign and since, I have tried to fill the gaps in my knowledge by asking those who witnessed events that I missed. In fact, since the campaign, I have reached out to those in my party as well as in other parties to clarify my understanding of certain events and to gain additional perspectives about what happened. Where I was present at meetings, I have quoted the speakers directly and described the scenes as I saw them. Where others told me of events and sayings, I have respected the requests of witnesses who preferred to be anonymous.

My goal is not to settle scores. Indeed, I have none to settle. It is to reflect on the people and events that made up the campaign as fairly as possible and to hope that scholars, practicing politicians and lay-people can all learn something from this. Where someone is portrayed in a bad light, I have tried where possible, to incorporate that person's or different perspectives.

Particularly, I hope the discussions resulting from this will help the NPP discover our mistakes, learn from them and thus be victorious in 2012.

I thank the NPP and particularly Nana Addo Dankwa Akuffo-Addo for giving me a chance to participate in this campaign.

There were many who doubted the wisdom of my inclusion in the campaign and therefore opposed it. I am grateful that he and others stood firmly behind me. I hope that in retrospect, my role will be appreciated.

No one can go through such an experience without coming to respect what politicians go through and how interested people are in this country.

My experience left me with diminished respect for some, enhanced appreciation for a few and a better appreciation for the challenges of politics and government in our challenging environment.

A book about an unsuccessful campaign is a difficult one to write. Despite the natural tendency to see enterprises in which one is involved in very positive terms, doing so in this case begs the question of why we lost. Thus failures and mistakes get more attention than the things that were done right. On the other hand, we must resist the temptation to be overly pessimistic. This is an election that would have been seen differently if half of one percent of the nearly 9 million who voted in the second round had voted differently.

My philosophical approach to politics is that we should strive for balance; of people, of groups and of ideas. It is obvious that the best way to build our democracy is to reach, always for the sensible centre.

The politics of confrontation and polarization will not lead us anywhere.

It is clear to me that currently and for years to come, no party in Ghana can win elections on its own. Elections will be determined by floating voters and floating regions.

I know that there are many who will be concerned about such a book. They fear that it will "wash our dirty linen in public". My response is that refusing to put out the truth will leave, out there, mostly lies. I hope this book will help our party and our country to move forward.

ARTHUR KENNEDY

CHAPTER ONE
THE STATE OF THE NATION

"Ask not what your country can do for you—ask what you can do for your country"

Former US President John F. Kennedy in his 1961 Inaugural Address

As the nation prepared to vote in 2008, there were a number of factors that pointed to trouble on the horizon despite the undoubted success of the New Patriotic Party (NPP) government in the administration of the country.

The NPP government had compiled a very enviable record that should have ensured the re-election of any incumbent government.

In the first place, the size of the economy had quadrupled from about 4 to 16 billion USD from 2001 to 2007 while inflation and interest rates declined.

Secondly, extreme poverty had dropped from 39.2% to 28.9%. This clearly showed that the changes in the economy had benefited significant numbers of poor people.

Thirdly, we had introduced the National Health Insurance Scheme that had, according to NHIS officials, given 11.7 million Ghanaians access to health for the first time since the Nkrumah's era. To add to this, the President had secured funding from the British government to support free maternal care for the next decade.

Fourth, new investments in education had increased enrollment at all levels of our educational system. Primary School enrollment, spurred by the Capitation Grant and School Feeding Program had increased by a third. Furthermore, enrollment in Public Universities had doubled while that in the Polytechnics had gone up by half.

Fifth, the NPP Government had undertaken a level of infrastructural constructions that had given us a superb network of roads. Many roads, like the Bole-Bamboi, Madina-Mamfe and the Mallam-Kasoa roads had been completed and many others were under construction.

Lastly, giant strides had been made in our freedom. The "CRIMINAL LIBEL LAW" had been repealed and many agreed that freedom had never had a more reliable friend than the NPP government.

Despite these formidable achievements, there were dark clouds on the horizon.

First, the government had come into office pledging "zero-tolerance" for corruption and in the judgment of many, had failed to deliver. Despite dealing promptly with the Mallam Issah case and passing some anti-corruption laws, many felt that the vim had gone out of the NPP government's anti-corruption crusade.

Second, many of our Ministers and functionaries had become too big for their breeches. Too many lived ostentatiously or dealt with people in a manner they did not appreciate. Perhaps, the group that in the public's mind exemplified this attitude the most were the District, Municipal and Metropolitan Chief Executives.

Third, despite the economic progress, we had not been able to create enough jobs and many were complaining that there was "no money in our pockets".

Fourth, despite the significant increase in the strength of the police, there was a perception that the crime rate had gone up.

Fifth, in 2007, the NPP had held a Presidential primary that had offended the sensibilities of many in its display of opulence. Then in 2008, we topped this off with a Parliamentary primary that was acrimonious and led to significant divisions in our party.

Sixth, there was a global economic downturn that was making all incumbents unpopular. This downturn had led to significant increases in the prices of fuel and food that had led to demonstrations in many developing nations, including Egypt, Haiti and Zambia.

Seventh, there was the natural itch for change that had worked for the NPP in 2000 but was working against us in 2008. After eight years, people wanted change.

Eighth, there were policies, initiated or not stopped in 2008 that tended to reinforce the perception that the NPP government was arrogant and uncaring. Amongst these were the failure to reduce the price of petrol significantly, the agreement to purchase presidential jets and the construction of the Jubilee House.

Ninth, the President and the party insisted on the resignation of about eight Senior Minister who were contesting for the party's nomination for the Presidency, depriving the government of some of the best talents in the party. To compound this, the President sacked the National Security Co-ordinator, Mr Francis Poku.

Within the ranks of the NDC, there appeared to be a determination to hold on to what they had.

As usual, there were a lot of voters who did not identify with either party and their votes were going to be crucial in determining the winners of both the Parliamentary and Presidential elections.

Even though the NDC had picked Professor John Evans Atta Mills in 2006, it appeared that he had been rather quiet since his nomination. Apparently, he had spent most of the time after his nomination building bridges to Central and Western Regions and ironing out the kinks in his campaign team.

One factor that played to the advantage of the NDC Candidate was the perception that he had been around the block enough times and deserved it this time. Ironically, the rumours about Prof. Mill's health got him more sympathy.

In retrospect, the signs of impending danger were clearly there if we cared to notice.

Petty traders in Accra and Kumasi were up in arms about being moved from their places of business without adequate plans for alternative places to hawk their wares.

Drivers were up in arms about harassment by the police and could not get relief till it was too late.

And within the NPP, foot-soldiers were complaining to all who cared to listen about their neglect by party and government functionaries.

During the heat of the campaign, we found a public that gave us some credit for what we had done but blamed us for what we had failed to do.

As former U.S. President Bill Clinton used to say "elections are always about the future". The public were going to judge us on what we would do in future, not what we had done in the past. Ironically, our mistakes, which were more recent, counted more with the public than the NDC/PNDC mistakes in the past. As a friend who described himself as an independent reminded me "Doc, we voted for your party in 2000 because of these same NDC mistakes and we are not going to vote for you again on the basis of the same mistakes."

CHAPTER TWO
THE STATE OF THE PARTY

"Your party is in the air but not on the ground"

Anonymous

HEADING INTO 2008, THE NPP WAS a pale shadow of the much-vaunted machine that had won the 2000 election. This had occurred gradually and was due to a number of factors.

WEAKENING THE PARTY

Many of the leaders who had led the party to victory chose to move into government. The most glaring examples of these were the National Chairman, Hon. Odoi Sykes, who resigned to be the Ambassador to Canada and the General Secretary, Dan Botwe, who resigned to be Minister of Information in 2005. With these resignations came a shifting of the centre of gravity from the party to the government.

During the first term of President Kufuor's administration, there were repeated complaints by party members that they were being neglected. This neglect involved party members who were by-passed for appointments or contracts and those who felt that power had created a chasm between them and their leaders. These feelings were exacerbated by the feeling that quite a number of people who had not toiled for the party were now in prominent positions. During the first term, many accepted the Presidency's explanation that the party would be the focus of the second term and that they would be taken care of. These feelings of alienation accounted for the rejection of the President's candidate for National Chairman, Stephen Ntim and the election of Peter Mac Manu et al as protest candidates.

When these protest candidates were elected, it portended a rocky relationship between the party and the Presidency. Unfortunately, the protest candidates who became executives were unable to redress the frustrations which had gotten them elected in the first place. In effect, the party voted against the President's candidates but was unable to wean itself off dependence on the Presidency.

In quite a number of regions, the teams that had helped us win in 2000 and 2004 were replaced with less competent teams. One very telling example of this was the Central Region where the new team never seemed to click the way the old one did. Most people in the party agree that in retrospect, the team led by Dr Kweku Ghartey was more effective that the one led by Danquah Smith, which replaced it in 2005. Another such place was in Ashanti where the new team led by Yaw Amankwaah never attained the prestige of the previous team led by Antoh.

One significant by-product of the election was that the NPP was saddled with a Chairman and General Secretary who, in addition to lacking the experience of their predecessors, could not work together. Indeed, for all the time that they have served together, the Chairman and the General Secretary have never had a consistent and professional working relationship. Repeated mediation efforts have been unsuccessful.

It was against this background that the Presidential Primary was waged. The primary brought issues of money and personality differences into the ranks of executives who were already divided. Some contend that these divisions were created in the first place by Presidential aspirants jockeying for early advantage by supporting candidates for constituency, regional and national office. As money flowed from candidates to party functionaries based on who supported who, the party became more divided and interested in money.

Party executives stopped building the party and took to trooping to Accra for contracts or hand-outs from big party men.

In many regions and constituencies, the 2005 elections and its aftermath led to deep-seated divisions between executives that left the party paralysed. For example, in the Volta Region, the factions were so entrenched that all the repeated efforts to reconcile them were unsuccessful.

As one Reverend Minister kept reminding me "Doc, your party is in the air but not on the ground."

This point was brought home dramatically when in June, 2008, at a meeting in Koforidua, the Campaign asked the National Chairman to request an audit of polling station executives. Though called an "audit", this was really supposed to be an inventory which would have indicated to the campaign the state of our grass-roots. It would have indicated which polling station executives were in place, which ones had died or moved away and which ones were active. Those in place and active were to be the back-bone of the party's grass-roots effort. Surprisingly, the National Chairman was unable to complete this audit before the elections. As he explained to me recently, the constituency officers just ignored his repeated requests for the information.

CAMPAIGN RESOURCES

On top of this, after what appeared to be a very expensive Parliamentary primary, many of the Parliamentary candidates did not have sufficient resources to begin campaigning on their own. Thus they stayed at home for critical months when they should have been pounding the pavement and knocking on doors to win support. In some instances, when the National campaign finally made resources available, candidates chose to pay off debts incurred during the primary or buy personal items. This bred suspicion and led to accusations and counter-accusations amongst party leaders and Parliamentary candidates. This situation was compounded by diminished volunteerism in the party. People wanted to be paid for everything they did for the party and there was simply not enough money to do that. I recall being visited by a lady party activist in Accra who complained that she and her friends wanted to help but were not getting the necessary resources to do so. I asked her to bring me a proposal for house-to-house campaigning by the four friends that would cover two polling stations. They had a budget of 10 thousand Ghana cedis for the two-day exercise! To be fair, many did not do these things to deliberately cause defeat. They believed in their hearts that the party would win and that since others were making money, they would do so too.

KUFUOR AND ALAN

The last piece of this saga was supplied by the President's decision to back Alan instead of stay neutral. Before her death, Hawa Yakubu had dramatically turned to the President at a party event and pleaded with him not to take sides in the Primary but the President had ignored that advice.

I remember meeting Dr Richard Anane, a close confidant of the President in the middle of 2007 at a funeral. I had worked with him during my NUGS Presidency and had a very good relationship with him. He said that politics in our party would always be reducible to a struggle between the Busia and Danquah factions. He felt that even though we were back together, the divisions that had cost Victor Owusu the elections of 1979 were still there. He felt that in the forthcoming primary, that struggle between the two factions was at play with Alan and Nana Addo representing the Busia and Danquah factions respectively.

When I asked him what he thought the President had learned from Ntim's defeat he said the President had learned that "he did not back Ntim enough and that if he wanted to go in and support a candidate, he should do so more decisively to ensure success". He said in the President's judgement, which he shared, Alan would make the best President amongst our crop of candidates and that the women would vote for him because of his looks. He said that in his view, a person who had never been in government could never be President. He also said that in his view, the President had never received sufficient credit for his stewardship. He revealed, for example that when the President decided to take the country to HIPC, virtually everybody in the cabinet, including the Finance Minister was against it."Yet after he hadasked for alternatives and they could provide none, he did it because he knew it was the right thing to do". Another such Kufuor loyalist is Maxwell Jumah, AKA, Kofi Ghana, who once introduced President Kufuor in New York by declaring that "I worship the ground Kufuor walks on". Despite the talk of the Danquah and Busia factions, the divisions are not as firm as they appear. According to Nana Addo, it was Danquah who handed the leadership of the party to Busia upon realizing that he had been tarnished by Nkrumah's propaganda to a point that made him ineffective. Also, despite talk of divisions, Victor Owusu had passed on to Nana Addo, his law chambers.

CHAPTER THREE
THE NPP PRESIDENTIAL AND
PARLIAMENTARY PRIMARRIES

"So dad, how did the election go?"

My son, Kwamina Kennedy, the day after the primary

THE NPP PRESIDENTIAL PRIMARY HAS BEEN described by many as too long, too extravagant and with too many candidates. They were right on all three counts.

INITIAL CAMPAIGN TEAM

I started considering a run for the slot in early 2005. My team and I felt that given the frustrations with Ministers, a new face could do very well. Furthermore, we surmised that even if I did not get very far, my ideas would get far and I would establish a foot-hold for the future.

It appeared to us that the most likely support bases would be the youth, Central and Western Regions and the party in the Diaspora.

I had groups of supporters in Toronto, Atlanta, Washington D.C. and London. We organized fund-raising events in all these places that were very well attended. I attended all the events except for the one in London. Also, we launched a website to publicise my ideas and our campaign manifesto. This web-site was very ably set up and ran by Dr and Mrs Akwasi and Akosua Boateng, of Little Rock, Arkansas. They put in incredible hours in support of the campaign and were just wonderful. The groups included quite a number of people in the Diaspora. Amongst these were Patrick Akenteng, Bellinia Asiedu-Young, Chris Yeboah and Isaac Asiedu of Toronto, Gus Mensah, Kojo Acquaah Harrison, Siaw, AKA Afro and Steve Biko of London, Sam Adofo and George Mensah of Atlanta, as well as Okyere Bona and Stephen Ofori-Appiah of Charlotte and Washington D.C. respectively.

In November of 2005, we organized an event at the University of Cape Coast to in effect, test the waters.

Right after this, we toured the Central region and were very encouraged by the response. Many were very happy to see "one of our own" in the race and pledged support. In fact, being from the Central Region was considered such an asset that quite a few other candidates started claiming links to the region, some of which were rather tenuous. Soon, we began touring the regions. I too played up my ties to other regions. I told audiences that though I hailed from the Central Region, I had been born in the Volta Region, educated in Ashanti and Greater Accra and had ties to Brong Ahafo Region by marriage. Wherever we visited, party members talked of their frustrations with "the establishment" and talked about how it was going to be "a new face".

Most of these tours lasted one to two weeks. To organize a tour, a team member or I would contact the regional party executives in a region to arrange for dates that would not conflict with those of other candidates. On arrival, we would map out the most cost-effective route based on the advice of local party leaders. Generally, we gave each party executive some money for transport.

In my message, I stressed my biography to emphasize that I was not a newcomer. I recounted my experiences as the NUGS President in the

1980's and how I became a two-time United Nation's Refugee as well as my service to the party while in exile. Furthermore, I talked about job-creation and sanitation. By far, however, the issue that had the most resonance was the neglect of foot-soldiers by the government and party leaders. My speeches were based on the MANIFESTO developed with the help of a Global team of Ghanaians, including Dr. A.B.A. Prempeh, Dr. Yaw Okraku, Dr. La-Kumi, Dr. George Acquaah-Mensah, Kojo Acquaah-Harrison and many others. Dr. Prempeh, one of my teachers at the Ghana Medical School who had become a mentor and a friend, was the leader in putting together the manifesto. He went over every sentence and checked every fact and punctuation. He brought to this task an unrivalled knowledge of the Danquah-Busia tradition and a delightful appreciation for policy. The MANIFESTO was published as a contribution by Bismarck Badu, a childhood friend.

I was accompanied by Kingsley Karikari, Gus Mensah, Twumasi-Kankam, Patrick Akenteng and Justice Opoku Fodjour on various legs of these tours. In most regions, the regional party executives would detail someone to accompany us on our tour. These activities were very ably co-ordinated by Dr. Kofi Barimah of the Catholic University who served as the National Campaign Co-ordinator.

We felt very encouraged by the reaction of party members to our efforts.

We toured all 230 constituencies about twice and some regions, a few more times.

While many party executives were just there to socialize, some were very good and serious. Amongst these were a number of Chairpersons from Greater Accra—Dr Odonkor of Ashiaman, Kwakufio Peterson of Kpone-Katamanso and Harold Opata of Shai-Osudoku. Another who impressed me was the Chair of Essikado-Ketan. They asked very good questions and were very respected by their executives.

I remember one evening early in the campaign when the Chair of Greater Accra region, Sammy Crabbe, organized for me to speak to some selected activists and intellectuals. It was a very enjoyable evening both for me and the audience.

WARNINGS OF FAILURE

Despite the euphoria surrounding our campaign, there were warnings of impending disaster.

The first was from AmoAsante, a resident of Washington D.C. When he met me in 2006 in Washington, he was very blunt. "Arthur K, you have brilliant ideas but those folks in Ghana do not care about ideas one bit. In the end, what will matter is money and even your relatives and friends will take money from someone else and abandon you in a moment."

My wife's concerns were heartfelt. "I know you want the best for your country but you must be cautious. I am concerned that in the end, many of those urging you on will not be with you to see this through to the end."

When I got to Ghana, my friend Dr. Adusei took me out. He said I was not going to do well but that I should have the commitment to build on what I was starting.

In the end, seventeen candidates contested the Presidential primaries, with the exception of Captain (Rtd.) Nkrabeah Effah-Darteh, who was disqualified.

It started with aspirants touring the constituencies and the regions to announce their intentions. Very early into the contest, aspirants started distributing gifts, sometimes monetary and at other times, non-monetary.

Newspapers lined up behind particular aspirants and against other aspirants.

In the early days, it seemed Professor Mike Ocquaye and Osafo Maafo were the front-runners but as time wore on, it began to look increasingly more and more like Nana Akufo-Addo or Alan Kyerematen.

As we prepared for the vetting, there were rumours that some would be disqualified and we went through possible questions over and over again.

PRE-VETTING MEETINGS

One day, before the vetting, I received a call from Honourable Odoi Sykes inviting me to a meeting to evaluate the campaign process to date. However, during the meeting, the then National Security Coordinator, Mr. Francis Poku, was in the Chair as we filed into the room. When I went in, he and others said they wanted to know how the campaign was going. Furthermore, they said there had been concerns about speculations that the President was supporting an aspirant and that they wanted to know my impressions about that.

During questioning, Professor Baddoe, who had taught me twenty-five years earlier at the Ghana Medical School wanted to know why I had not returned to Ghana earlier if I planned to contest the Presidency in the future. They thanked me and wished me well.

ASPIRANTS MEET PRESIDENT KUFUOR

As a follow-up to the meeting, we were invited to meet the President.

The President said that while he had a preference amongst the aspirants, he had not gone out of his way to use state resources to support that candidate. The President reminded the gathering that as far back as 1998, Alan Kyerematen had considered contesting for the Presidency against him. During discussions, there were forceful exchanges of views on the President's perceived support for a particular candidate. The high point of the meeting was Jake Obetsebi Lamptey statement that while he welcomed the President's pledge to discipline government officials who use their positions to support particular candidates, it appeared to him that this rule was applied rather selectively.

The President asked for an example and Jake supplied it. The President in turn also expressed misgivings about allegations that Jake Obetsebi Lamptey claimed to have brought him from obscurity to the Presidency, which was denied by Jake.

In response to a point made by Kwabena Agyapong, the President asked "Kwabena, whom did you support in 98?" After Kwabena indicated that he had supported Nana Akufo-Addo, the President said "Afterwards, did I not bring you into my government? Sometimes, we should give credit where it is due."

While the President seemed irritated at times, he seemed to have come prepared for an honest airing of the relevant issues. Unfortunately, except for Jake Obetsebi Lamptey and a few others, we chose not to engage the President seriously.

Neither Alan Kyerematen nor Nana Akufo-Addo said anything during the meeting.

ALAN UNSCRIPTED

As I walked out after the meeting, Alan Kyerematen pulled me aside. We had a very informative one hour chat, standing on the steps, in front of the castle. He felt that he had worked very hard to get to his current position and was not being given due credit for his hard work. When I asked about the fund-raiser that was raising eye-brows, he said that all the money had come from businessmen who believed he would be a very good President and wanted to support him. He had put on the fund-raiser to show the party that he could raise money. He indicated that he believed that during the primaries, others had spent more than he had. I asked Alan whether he would agree that there was no co-ordination within the government with respect to the NPP primary contest. He agreed and suggested that if the kind of co-ordination I was referring to had been done, he would have been the choice of many Ministers. He felt his critics were motivated by pettiness and envy. When he said that, I asked whether in view of what he had just said, he could unite the party if he were the nominee. He said he had no doubt that he could unite the party and that "once the voting is over, everyone will bow to reality". He assured me that his relationship with all the other Ministers running were very cordial. He was very animated but very friendly and cordial as we talked that evening.

As I was to find out in my subsequent interactions with him, contrary to the public perception, Alan talks quite a bit.

VETTING COMMITTEE

Before the meeting with the President, there was the Vetting Committee.

Before the vetting, there were many rumours that many candidates would be disqualified. These rumours were heightened when there were reports that Alan had trouble with them and that Vice-President had a scheduling mis-understanding.

When I walked in, Chairman Peter Ala Adjetey quickly put me at ease. He said they were there to be sure I had all the required documents. Once they were satisfied that I had the needed documents, we settled down to chat about the Presidency and how I would handle it. The Chairman went round the table and members asked questions. They ranged from picking cabinet Ministers to relations with the party etc. The members were all very polite and their questions were very good.

When Peter asked me how I ended up in exile and I said towards the end of my answer that I had been inspired by listening to him once in Madina while I was a student. He said "Ah, so you learned to open your mouth too wide eh?" The room erupted in laughter.

PRIMARY ALLIANCES

Many have asked why so many aspirants stayed in till the end and whether there could have been any alliances amongst the aspirants. I believe that so many of us stayed in because the party delegates gave all of us the impression that we were doing well. As to why there were no alliances, I think there were a lot of discussions amongst various aspirants about alliances. On my part, after repeated encouragement from some friends and party members, I had separate meetings and discussions with Mr. Boakye Agyarko, Dr. Kofi Konadu Apraku, and Professor Frimpong Boateng.

Even before returning to Ghana, I had spoken with Boakye Agyarko. Some mutual friends suggested that since we were good friends and had similar ideas, it would seem reasonable to explore merging our campaigns. When I called Boakye, while he was very polite, he felt it was premature to discuss alliances at that point.

The most productive of those conversations was with Professor Frimpong Boateng. We even discussed the outline of a method for determining who would step down and tentatively picked a mediator who would help us implement the process. I think time simply run out on our discussions.

I also had a very good meeting with Dr Apraku who said that BNI surveys had him ahead of the pack. When I said I had been briefed of the same polls but they had others ahead, he disputed that.

In addition to these, I had a very interesting conversation with Honourable Kennedy Agyapong, representing the Nana Addo campaign and discussed endorsement scenarios if the vote was to go for a second round and some interesting running-mate scenarios. Some have asked whether the number of candidates could have been limited either through these voluntary alliances or by the party. The answer is yes. The President, in particular could have facilitated a process for limiting the number of Ministers who ran. When he was urged to do so, he is reported to have replied that he could not because he was not trusted as an honest broker. He felt that if he launched such an initiative, it would be interpreted as an attempt to garner support for Alan.

With time running out, I almost got the break that would have lifted my candidacy to the front ranks. I heard that party elder Apenteng Appiah-Menkah was about to short-list five of the seventeen aspirants and that I would be one of the five. In a meeting later at his office in Accra, he confirmed that I would be on his list of five which would be released two weeks before the vote. We felt that this would suddenly give me more airtime and significantly improve my ability to raise money.

Unfortunately, he was persuaded not to release that list of five.

Many of my initial assumptions proved to be not well founded. Many friends who had pledged support turned out to be unsupportive while others I had never met turned out to be very supportive. Some who pledged support had pledged support to others as well.

I remember a lady who had been introduced to me by a friend in Accra. On my very first visit to her, she made it clear that she was unwavering in her commitment to Nana Akufo-Addo. "But I will help you because people like you deserve to be encouraged since you represent the future." True to her word, she not only made a contribution but arranged for others to do so too. Every few weeks, she would call and arrange for sponsorship for me.

During the primaries, the most insightful advice I got was from a Ghanaian official with the World Bank who urged me not to attack anybody but to stay on course. "I know as the primaries get nearer, they will be a tendency for some of you to go after the President. However, he is not one of your opponents so leave him out as much as possible."

ELECTION DAY

The night before the primary, there was frenzied wooing of the delegates by candidates.

During the voting, the lobbying continued, culminating in the "Lord Commey" incident.

NPP aspirants on Primary Day, Dec. 23rd, 2007

Since then, there have been a lot of debates about what happened that day at Legon. What was Paul Affoko doing? Was he sharing money or was he frame? Were there others too?

Following the incident, voting was halted and there was an emergency meeting of aspirants with the National Chairman. There were heated exchanges. The Vice-President complained about District Chief Executives (DCE) ignoring him at best or openly defying him because they had been directed to support another candidate. He asked rhetorically "I am the Vice-President or not?" Alan Kyerematen denied that those sharing the money, as alleged by Lord Commey, were his supporters. Peter Mac Manu swore that he was not going to "allow anybody to disrupt my congress". In the end, the meeting decided to let the voting proceed with the understanding that the "Lord Commey" incident would be investigated. As is well-known, after the first round, Alan Kyerematen conceded and Nana Akufo-Addo became the nominee by consensus.

President Kufuor and NPP aspirants right after primaries in Accra.

To my shock and bewilderment, I got one vote.

In the days after the primary when I really felt depressed, my spirits were lifted by calls from the many young people who called to urge me to hang in.

How could this happen after all the pledges from Wenchi delegates? "Doctor, if you get ten votes, you should know they are the votes from Wenchi. If Patrick is your friend, then you are one of us". There were similar pledges from places like Sawla in the Northern Region, parts of Brong Ahafo and Central Region. Some would voluntarily invite me home and pledge in front of their families, without any prompting, to vote for me. The extent of deception, of virtually all candidates, was breath-taking.

In the end, they chose the best candidate, in their judgment, guided by the broader interest of the party.

The rules of the party governing the Presidential Primaries were flouted repeatedly without consequences. The attitude of the National Executive was that things would take care of themselves. This "see no evil, hear no evil" would haunt us all through the 2008 campaign. A key example was the requirement that party executives refrain from endorsing any aspirants. While Abena Kwala, the Western Regional Women's Organizer, consistent with this rule, resigned to support Honourable Papa Owusu Ankomah, many others supported some aspirants without bothering to resign and nothing happened. In the end, one of the few who dealt honestly with me throughout was Alhaji Gibrine, the Regional Organizer for Central Region. He always told me that while he would help get anything done that I asked, he was also helping other candidates the same way.

MEMORIES FROM PRIMARIES

Amongst the many experiences, a few stand out. I can still recall Gus Mensah, of London, mile after mile on the road, singing hymn after hymn, as we travelled for days on end, bringing back memories of hymns long forgotten.

Second, there was that day in the Northern Region when our one-car convoy, caught fire as we travelled from Karaga to Gushiegu. Luckily, this happened in front of a group of workers who quickly put out the flames with sand and got us an electrician to fix the problem for us.

Third, we ate in so many chop bars that we could have written a very respectable guide to chop-bars. Perhaps, my most memorable meal was eating "Oyuo soup" in a chop bar near Axim one Saturday morning. The favourites for home-cooked meals is between eating some banku and okro stew prepared by Mrs Blagodgie, the wife of the Volta Youth Organizer, Maxwell Bladgodgie on a breezy evening at Nkwanta and tuo-safe prepared by Auntie Vic, the Women's Organizer for Yarpei-Kusagu, in Bolga. I get hungry just thinking of those meals.

My fourth image is the day we were travelling to Chereponi and got lost. After driving for some time, we saw a woman by the roadside and stopped to ask her for directions. As soon as we stopped near her, she threw down her cutlass and started running towards the village. Since we did not know what she was going to say, we drove away quickly.

NPP PRIMARIES

As the Parliamentary primaries got under way, Nana Akufo-Addo indicated to the campaign team that he did not intend to meddle in it.

It became quickly apparent, however, that the shadow of the Presidential primary would affect the primaries. Soon there were reports of primary candidates identifying themselves as Nana Akufo-Addo's or Alan Kyerematen's candidates. As if this was not bad enough, the regional and national executives got involved in ways that were generally not helpful. In some places, candidates who appeared qualified were disqualified for strange reasons to smooth the path of their opponents while others who were not qualified were cleared and shepherded to victory. Even in places where proper primaries had been held, the results were bitterly disputed. These disputed primaries led to fights in the streets between our supporters and on-air disagreements between party leaders that cost our party crucial support. For example, while the National Chairman Peter Mac Manu and the Regional Chairman, Sammy Crabbe, traded accusations and insults on air over the primaries in Greater Accra, the National Chairman and General Secretary were also giving conflicting directives over some constituencies in Ashanti,.

The result of all these was that we had an unprecedented number of independent candidates. Though a number of them won, they cost us crucial support in many places and sent our candidates down to defeat. Notable examples were Yendi and Salaga where we lost seats.

Many believe that losing our Parliamentary majority in the first round contributed significantly to losing the Presidential elections in the second round.

CHAPTER FOUR
ASSEMBLING THE CAMPAIGN TEAM

"They were a collection of stars but not a team"

Anonymous

THE PRESIDENTIAL CANDIDATE FACED SIGNIFICANT PROBLEMS in assembling his team. Furthermore, he was determined to avoid his own experience after the 1998 elections when he had felt marginalized.

On January,3rd, 2008, the Presidential candidate invited all the former aspirants to breakfast.

After the pleasantries were over, Nana Akufo-Addo addressed the gathering.

He told all of us that he had sat where we were sitting before and knew how we felt. He too, had lost a primary before and had felt disappointed. What mattered, however, was the team. He said he had played soccer before and that any successful team had stars. "As captain of our team, I am happy to have bright stars on the team because it will help us win. I know that the captain always gets to lift the trophy."

"He urged all of us to get on board and help the NPP win the 2008 election. When he opened the floor for comments many pledged support and offered advice.

Boakye-Agyarko and Alan Kyerematen argued a little about economic growth and job-creation, with both making very good points on why we had not done so well and how we could do it better.

On the whole, it was a very good start to building a united team.

It is reported that there was a heated debate within Nana Akufo-Addo's inner circle as well as with party leaders on key campaign appointments.

The party is reported to have pushed for Dan Botwe as Campaign Director while others pushed for Jake Obetsebi Lamptey. Others also felt that the old system of just having a Campaign Manager should be maintained. In the end, the candidate and the party leadership opted for a multi-tier structure. The candidate appointed Dr. Kofi Konadu-Apraku as Director and Jake Obetsebi-Lamptey as Chairman. His Deputies were Mr. Roland Saka for the Northern Sector and Ms Sophia Horner Sam, for the Southern Sector.

First, there was supposed to be a coordinating structure made up of the President, the Candidate, the National Chairman and the Chairman of the Council of Elders. It was understood that most of the time; the Chief of Staff, Mr. Kwadwo Mpiani would represent the President.

Below this was the Campaign Committee. This was made up of the Chairpersons of the various campaign Committees, the National Executives of the party and Honourable Yaw Osafo Maafo, Hajia Rukaya Ahmed and Ms Mawuse Awittey.

To the side was the Committee of Aspirants, which was made up of all aspirants and was to serve in an advisory capacity to the campaign committee. After the initial meeting, the committee of aspirants was never convened again.

Each Chairperson had a committee, whose members had been chosen in advance to work with. My impression after the first meeting was that each committee, based on its terms of reference, was to work and report to the Committee as a whole.

The following were the Committee Chairpersons,

1: MANIFESTO	DR. OWUSU AFRIYIE AKOTO
2: FUNDRAISING	HON. HACKMAN OWUSU AGYEMANG, MP
3: SECURITY	HON. DR. KWAME ADDO KUFUOR, MP
4: COMMUNICATIONS	DR. ARTHUR KOBINA KENNEDY
5: IDENTIFIABLE GROUPS	HON. ALAN KYEREMATEN
6: ELECTORAL AFFAIRS	MR. DAN BOTWE
7: OPERATIONS	MR. NICH ADI-DAKU
8: RESEARCH	MR VICTOR NEWMAN
9: TRADITIONAL AFFAIRS	HON. FELIX OWUSU AGYAPONG, MP

Each Chairperson had a committee selected in advance and terms of reference, developed by its chair in collaboration with Dr Apraku.

Soon after the Campaign Committee was announced, it became apparent that there was a management committee whose membership was not announced and which operated by invitation only. The Committee was to execute campaign committee decisions and to make interim decisions that the committee would ratify.

Naturally, for such a large number of committees, there was overlapping responsibilities.

Research and Communication both dealt with information-gathering while Election Affairs and Operations had a lot in common.

Also, Chieftaincy Affairs and Identifiable groups had a bit in common.

The Committees were left to organize their own activities either in response to assignments by the campaign committee or on their own initiative.

For such a system to work, there needed to be a high degree of collaboration and trust amongst a large group of people and as the next chapter demonstrates, this was very difficult to attain.

Nana addresses Press with NPP leaders. From Rt. To Lt. Jake, McManu, Hackman Owusu Agyemang.

Of course, this was not the whole team. We needed teams in the regions and the districts. Also, this was not just a Presidential campaign. It was also a Parliamentary campaign and we needed to integrate the campaigns of all our Parliamentary candidates with that of the presidential candidate.

Later on, the composition of the team became an issue when Alan Kyerematen resigned. It was felt that he had not been given a position influential enough or commensurate with his status. As many of us learned during the campaign, it really did not matter much what your title was. What mattered was one's access to the candidate and the support of those making the spending decisions. While more consultation would probably have helped, Alan Kyerematen could have made something of anything he was given.

Alan submitted his resignation letter to the party Chairman on Thursday, April 17th. According to the "Daily Graphic" the resignation was due to harassment of some of his supporters who wanted to contest the NPP Parliamentary primaries. On Monday, the 21st of April, the "Daily Graphic" published a statement signed by Jake Obetsebi-Lamptey from the campaign team expressing regret at the resignation. It revealed that a few days before the resignation, Nana Akufo-Addo had visited Alan to discuss his concerns and the future of the party. The statement concluded that the party had always been bigger than any individual and hoped that wiser counsel would prevail for Alan to return. On Thursday, April 24th, following reports that Alan was back, he issued a statement re-affirming his resignation. He said he had been asked by Mr. Da Rocha to withdraw his resignation before his concerns were addressed and that he disagreed with that approach. He stated that "We must also not lose sight of the fact that national interest is superior to the interest of any single party." With that, Mr Da Rocha issued a statement saying that the NPP should let Alan go. "It is my considered view that it will not be in the best interest of the NPP to receive Mr Kyerematen back into the party's fold." Mr Da Rocha concluded that " I am not convinced that the matters he complained about are so grave, so earth-shaking as to make a loyal party member quit it unceremoniously and I told him so."

With regards to Alan Kyerematen's resignation, I know there are many who felt the NPP should have called his bluff and allowed him to leave the party but I strongly disagree. I remember the anger that greeted his resignation. Party elder da Rocha's call for the NPP to "let him go" had a lot of support.

Initially, I also shared in the anger but changed my mind for two reasons. First, I spoke to Mr. Appiah Menkah who impressed me very much with his commitment to maintaining our unity. He recounted how in 1979, as the UNC broke away from the PFP, many who could have worked to bring back the break away faction ridiculed them and underplayed their influence. As is well-known that cost us the 1979 election and may have contributed to the instability leading to a decade of military rule.

As he himself readily acknowledged, Alan Kyerematen's departure would not be as significant as the UNC split but it was unhelpful to have him leave. The second factor that changed my mind was that the week-end before it was resolved, I was in Kumasi to attend a funeral. Without any prompting, many ordinary party members brought it up. While they vehemently condemned Alan Kyerematen for quitting in the middle of an election campaign, they all invariably ended up appealing to leadership to work hard towards returning Alan Kyerematen to the fold. In a statement issued by the National Chairman, the party welcomed Alan back. It announced the establishment of a six-member committee to look into his concerns. In the end, not much was heard of that committee and the campaign resumed after wasting valuable time in the middle of the campaign. While his resignation was inappropriate, his return was a good thing.

I know there are some who think he should be disqualified from contesting the next leadership race because of that episode. I believe that when the party asked him to withdraw his resignation, it did not ask him to return with limited rights. Therefore, he should be presumed to be a long-standing party member with the same rights as if he never resigned. Obviously, those voting for a leader are entitled to consider any number of issues, including this issue in deciding who they would vote for if Alan Kyerematen were to run.

Alan greets Nana during NPP Rally.

CHAPTER FIVE
THE CAMPAIGN TEAM

" A committee is a cul-de-sac down which ideas are lured and then quietly strangled".

Anonymous

WHILE THERE WAS A LOT OF lobbying to get on the Campaign Committee, once the campaign started, it quickly became apparent that what mattered was access to the candidate and control of money. Given how large the committee was, co-ordination was going to be crucial to our success and those entrusted with this job would determine to a large extent, our success or failure.

After our initial meetings, we had a few other meetings, to discuss strategy and our performance. One of the things that created confusion was the change from using a Campaign Manager in 2000 and 2004, to using a Director and a Chairman for 2008.

The fissures in the team did not take long to surface.

When the team met for the second time, Nana Akufo-Addo informed the team that he wanted himself and Dr. Kofi Konadu Apraku to "be the pivots around which this campaign will revolve".

That statement was to have wide ramifications. Until then, most of us had not been clear about the campaign hierarchy. With that he seemed to be making it clear that Dr. Kofi Konadu Apraku would ran the show.

Soon after the inauguration of the campaign committee, it became obvious that many in the Party's national executive were not happy with their roles in the campaign. It appeared that despite being assigned to particular committees, they had expected to manage, not just be part of the work of the campaign. Of these, the unhappiest appeared to be the Women's Organizer, Mrs. Rita Asobayire and the National Organizer, Lord Commey. At most meetings, one could count on Rita getting up to give a long list of things not being done. This would invariably be supported strongly by Dan Botwe, seconded by Lord Commey. Nana Akufo-Addo would ask in exasperation" but you are all members of this committee. What is the problem?"

As Dan Botwe and the party functionaries saw it, the campaign was trying to re-invent the wheel too often. He pointed out repeatedly, "This is not the first time we are running a campaign. We have done this before." He felt that the party's structure and functionaries should be an integral part of everything. To those who shared that view, trying to set up parallel structures when the party structures were there and available to be used was only duplicating structures and wasteful. In my view, those put in charge of the campaign could have worked harder to integrate the party people into their activities. Many others and I watched in amazement as in meeting after meeting, we were told that Lord Commey had not been informed or involved in things planned and executed by the operations committee.

To be fair, sometimes the lack of involvement was due to party functionaries, sulking by themselves in the corner and hoping for things to go wrong so that they could complain. My committee had quite a number of people assigned to it who made it to very few of our meetings but always found time to complain about how they were not being involved. One such person was the General Secretary, Nana

Ohene Ntow. An expert in communication who obviously had a point of view and some skills, it was virtually impossible to get him to work with the committee on anything. To his credit, the National Chairman was always trying to heal the rifts between the campaign and the party executives. While I was not privy to what he told the candidate and Dr. Apraku in private, he was very supportive during meetings.

Interestingly, the tensions that existed between the campaign and the party were mirrored by that between the campaign and the government. The difference was that the complaints from the Ministers were muted. The Ministers complained that the campaign did things without their knowledge and that they had information that would improve the campaign. Since I was not privy to the meetings at the highest levels of the campaign and government functionaries, my view is necessarily limited by what I heard and saw. As far as my committee was concerned, Madam Oboshie Sai-Cofie was very easy to work with. She was always helpful and available if one needed help.

Unfortunately, Honourable Stephen Asamoah Boateng (Asabe) was in the beginning not very available. He did not attend meetings but would see the candidate often to give ideas. The result was that my committee was always being urged by the candidate to involve Asabe in our activities while we had difficulty reaching him. To be fair to him, he was a candidate and therefore needed to spend time in his constituency and this may have contributed to his lack of easy availability. Whenever he was available though, he was forceful and very aggressive about getting things done. Towards the end, Asabe was one of the hardest-working candidates. Even when he lost his seat, he worked very hard for the Presidential ticket in the second round. Many believed that in the election year, maintaining Oboshie at Information and sending Asabe to Local Government would have been ideal.

Outside the campaign, some of the most active were the Chief of Staff, Mr. Kwadwo Mpiani and the late Honourable Kwadwo Baah-Wiredu. The Chief of Staff was always accessible and helpful whenever anyone had concerns. When the President arranged a meeting between the government and the campaign to exchange information on the Manifesto, the late Kwadwo Baah-Wiredu was wonderful. At the retreat, I raised concerns about corruption in the administration of justice. When the Minister of Justice, Honourable Joe Ghartey rose in defense of the judiciary, it led to some interesting exchanges. I got support from some surprising quarters, including the Vice-President, the Chief of Staff and Honourable Paapa Owusu Ankomah, himself a former Attorney General. They told the Minister that my complaints were common knowledge. Generally, the discussions were very candid and very useful. Afterwards, I approached Hon. Baah Wiredu for help on simplifying our economic message and we spent countless hours refining and breaking down our message. A few days before he left, he asked that we meet to rap up that work. When we were unable to meet, we agreed to meet as soon as possible after his return to complete the task. Unfortunately, he never returned. Two Ministers and former aspirants who were really wonderful to work with were Dr. Addo Kufuor and Hon. Felix Owusu Agyapong. The former Defence Minister, before his return to government, was always accessible and helpful. Hon. Owusu Agyapong was an inexhaustible source of commonsense and good humour. I remember sitting next to him at a rally at Asamankese. He told me it was going to rain just around five p.m. and that every local person knew that. When it started raining as if on cue, he said "Doc, the problem with you young people is that you do not take advice. I told those planning the event that this time of the year, it rains almost everyday around five in the evening and that we should finish the rally by then. Unfortunately, they did not listen and here we are."

Talking about unity rallies, there was one addressed by a former aspirant and key member of the campaign. As was the norm then, he exhorted all in the party to unite behind Nana Akufo-Addo."Today, there is no Jake campaign, there is no Botwe campaign, there is no Alan campaign, and there is no Apraku campaign. There is only the Nana Addo campaign and the NPP campaign. Let us all unite behind it." As luck would have it, right after the rally, he ran into a lady who had taken money from him during the primary to support his campaign and he believed had supported Nana. As soon as the lady said "hello", he exploded "You took my money and voted for someone else! God will punish you for that. Mark my words."

Once during the campaign, Mrs. Chinery-Hesse convened a meeting at the President's behest. She indicated that the President desired better co-ordination between the government's communication team and that of the campaign. This was music to my ears. This meeting was attended by Jake Obetsebi Lamptey, Asabe, the National Chairman and the General Secretary. We agreed on the need to co-ordinate responses whenever there were evolving circumstances or breaking news. The meeting agreed that I would be the central point in this effort. Unfortunately, most of the things agreed to were not done. I remember trying to get information on the Vodafone deal for our communicators to go on air and defend the government. We were finding it difficult to get the very documents the NDC campaign had and were quoting from freely on air.

We had completed the meeting and were filing out when I asked Mrs. Chinery-Hesse what the President's role in the campaign was going to be. "Doc, the President will do whatever he is requested to do." I was to hear that phrase quite a few times before the end of the campaign.

Ironically, one person who fore-saw the need for enhancing team-work in the campaign was Jake Obetsebi Lamptey. The week-end after the inauguration of the team, Jake Obetsebi Lamptey invited a group of us, some from Nana Akufo-Addo's original campaign team, to bond. The meeting was not well-attended but he was trying to lay the groundwork for better collaboration. He started by thanking the old guard for accepting us on board and urged that we work together in the interest of the party and the candidate. He suggested that the group meet regularly to review the progress of the campaign. Unfortunately, the group never met again.

A few days into the campaign, I called Dr. Kofi Konadu Apraku about an issue and he indicated that he was not happy that "you are running to Jake Obetsebi Lamptey on everything. I am watching that." I was stunned. I thought we were a team and that dealing with Jake Obetsebi Lamptey would not be a problem. About a month later, I was invited to a meeting to discuss communication. Gabby Otchere Darko indicated those who had been invited and pointed out, quite appropriately that while Alhaji Harruna Atta was a member of our committee, he had failed to attend any meeting despite repeated invitations. After the discussion with Gabby Otchere Darko, I called Dr. Apraku to indicate my committee's concerns with not being involved in who to invite for a discussion of our work. I suggested that we should invite Madam Oboshie Sai Coffie, who despite being a Minister was always present at our meetings. Dr. Apraku did not take kindly to that. In the early period of the campaign, there were run-ins between the Campaign Director and quite a few of other key members of the campaign.

Sometimes, people were excluded from meetings without explanation. Once, Boakye-Agyarko was asked not to join a meeting by the Campaign Committee Secretary, Seratu, who claimed to be acting upon Dr. Apraku's instruction. Dr. Apraku was very hard-working but not collegial.

After the Regional Monitoring Team had been put in place, I complained during a Campaign Committee meeting that I had not been consulted in assembling the Central Region team, despite my position on the National Campaign Committee. To the amazement of virtually the entire committee, Jake Obetsebi Lamptey said "Well, I was not consulted about the composition of the Greater Accra team either". Here was the National Campaign Committee Chairman and three-time Chairman of Greater Accra admitting that he had not been consulted on the formation of his region's campaign team!

After the initial series of meetings, the Campaign Committee meetings became rather infrequent. Most of the time, the members of the team were spread all over the country.

Another difficulty that soon surfaced was that many in the campaign team decided that their priority was to be wherever the candidate happened to be, regardless of their own responsibilities. Thus, quite often, campaign officials needed for decision-making in Accra were invariably with the candidate on the road. There were some meetings in which the Campaign Director was asked pointedly whether he wanted to ran the campaign or follow the candidate.

THE SPENDING COMMITTEE

NPP Campaign team visits ALUWORKS

In addition to these difficulties, many of the committees that were established never functioned effectively. Sometimes, this was because the members lacked initiative. At other times, it was because their programs were not funded. This did not mean that their areas were not important. They were. It was just that sometimes others performing the same functions had better links to the Finance or better still, the Spending Committee.

Nobody was sure when and where the Spending Committee met. Regardless of whatever the Campaign Committee decided, the Spending Committee could make its own decisions as to what to fund and what not to fund, to the frustration and bewilderment of many.

This group, referred to sometimes as the Databank group included Kelly Gadzepo, Nana Ofori-Atta, Ken Ofori-Atta and others. They had their own way of determining what mattered to the campaign and what did not matter.

My committee, the Communication Committee kept sending advertising plan after plan which would be accepted and yet not funded. We repeatedly worked out procedures for developing and approving adverts but they never seemed to work. There always seemed to be others beyond our control and unaccountable to us, deciding advertising priorities. Thus while our committee had a lot of serious communication professionals, we never got a grip on communications as a group.

Some amongst the committee who had special links to the Spending Committee started developing adverts without reference to the committee and getting them on air without the agreement of the Communication Committee.

SPEECHWRITING

Personally, the area that I came to enjoy most was that of writing speeches. After some initial confusion, I was designated the primary speechwriter.

Our process of writing speeches was very interesting. If we had time, a committee of relevant experts on the subject would be convened with the candidate sitting in to discuss the outline of the speech. Afterwards, another committee would be designated to prepare a draft speech. I would often be asked to prepare the draft and then consult anybody I felt like talking to. It was great to work on speeches with the likes of Robert Ahomka-Lindsey, Alan Kyerematen, Dr. Apraku, Oboshie Sai

Cofie and Jake Obetsebi Lamptey. Sometimes, Elizabeth Ohene would join us.

After the draft, the group would reconvene to discuss the draft. Whenever someone was unhappy with something in a speech, I realized that they found it easier to disagree with the speech-writer rather than the candidate. One such occasion was when, together with Dr Owusu Afriyie Akoto, I did an estimate of the jobs that could be created and included that in a speech that was delivered. I was repeatedly taken to task by others who did not like the estimate. It did not matter to them that the candidate had quizzed Dr Afriyie and I to his satisfaction before permitting the inclusion of the estimate.

Invariably, the draft would get longer as people fought to add a paragraph here or a sentence there. Sometimes, this went on too long. One notable example was the IEA encounter when the process went on so long that the candidate was late for the speech.

My worst experience was when I prepared a draft speech for delivery to the Association of Ghana Industries. After consulting all those I was asked to consult, we held a meeting to discuss the speech.

Right at the beginning, Appiah Menka took the floor. "I like Arthur K" he said "but this draft is not good enough".

After some discussion, Alan Kyerematen came to my defense. "You know, he has everything we asked him to include but some of us have not read the entire draft." He suggested that I start using sub-headings so that people could easily identify their areas of interest. To be criticized that way by someone I respected so much was painful but I was assigned to rewrite the speech and when we re-assembled, he was wholesome in his praise of my effort.

The three speeches I enjoyed writing most were the ones on healthcare, to the IEA and on the Northern Development Authority. While the speeches were good, I felt they were too long but I always lost the fight to keep them short.

Nana Akufo-Addo was meticulous in making sure that all the punctuations and corrections were in the right place. Once, after staying up all night, I delivered a speech to him on my way to the office. By the time I got to the office, he had read it and was ready to discuss corrections. Interestingly, none of them was better received than the one he delivered to the Nigerian Bar Association in Abuja. He was repeatedly interrupted by applause and got a long standing ovation in the end.

I knew he had been a Marxist as a young university student but had not liked Nkrumah's excesses. Therefore, after the speech, I said many people thought his delivery sounded like Nkrumah. "Good God, Kennedy!" he said, amidst laughter by everybody.

SELECTING SPEAKERS/PANELISTS

To return to our committee, even the question of who to put on air when was never completely under our control. Indeed, initially, Dr. Kofi Konadu Apraku had very serious reservations about me appearing on air. While his opinion of me improved, it was very obvious that he preferred others as the face of our Communication group.

At some point, we made some effort to gain control of who would speak at rallies but that quickly collapsed. Before and during a rally, there would always be intense lobbying as to who would speak. Towards the end, that task was taken up by Lord Commey and Obiri. There was rarely a discussion of what the speakers would say. This penchant for putting microphones in people's hands and praying that they would say the right thing caused us quite a number of problems.

For example, in the Central Region, Grace Omaboe, popularly known as Maame Dokonu, in one of her flights of eloquence, revealed that "Nana Akufo-Addo is my brother and I am supporting him." While that would have been appropriate in a rally in the Eastern Region, it did not go over very well in the Central Region where Professor Mills hails from. Within days, NDC operatives had copies of the speech playing on virtually every station in the region to our distress, while others went from house to house urging Fantes to "follow Mame Dokono's example and help our brother Mills too."

Another such moment occurred when during the second round in Winneba, during an event meant to give the candidate a chance to interact with fisherman, Ms Christie Churcher suddenly went on her knees and started begging for forgiveness on behalf of the NPP. Needless to say, the NDC started telling people what crimes we were asking for forgiveness for. That moment was never scripted. It was spontaneous.

Many committees complained that they were not getting the resources they needed to do the work they had been assigned to do. Other such committees, with the exception of my own were the Identifiable Groups Committee and the Chieftaincy Affairs Committee. For example, after Alan Kyerematen rejoined the Campaign as a Special Advisor to Nana Akufo-Addo, the Committee under the leadership of Paapa Owusu Ankomah and Boakye Agyarko developed a very ambitious outreach program to settler communities that never got off the ground.

Towards the end, the Campaign Committee decided that something needed to be done about the manner in which the campaign was being run. The committee decided to establish, in place of the initial management committee, another one made up of committee chairmen. This group met twice a week. Under the leadership of Jake Obetsebi Lamptey, it helped to resolve some of the lingering issues in the campaign. The meetings were well attended and very business-like, initially. After some time, the key people in the campaign stopped showing up.

POOR CO-ORDINATION

The lack of effective co-ordination within the campaign spilled over into other areas. Towards the end, the lack of co-ordination was dramatically illustrated at a meeting in Kumasi. With the flag-bearer in attendance and the virtually all constituency executives in the region seated, the Campaign Director took the floor. He indicated that the meeting had been convened to resolve outstanding issues in the constituencies. Most of these were incidents that originated in the primaries. Dr. Apraku proceeded to give a blow-by-blow account of each of these conflicts. Some time into his presentation, some in the room indicated that the problems the meeting had been convened to discuss had already been resolved a week earlier.

It was then that it became apparent that the meeting had been convened without the involvement of the Chair of the Regional Campaign Committee, Honourable Kan Dapaah. When he finally got the microphone, Honourable Kan Dapaah was understated and very reasonable. He suggested that better consultation would have saved everybody a lot of time and effort. As he stated "Mobaa ye yi na yedii amannie a anka, mmre anssei (If we had had the customary conversation that visitors should have with their hosts when you arrived, we would have saved everyone a lot of time.)". It turned out that the week before, the Ashanti Region Campaign Committee had spent some time identifying the flashpoints in the region and set up a committee under the Chairmanship of Mr. Appiah-Menka to resolve the problems identified. The committee, most people accepted, had done a very good job of addressing the key issues in most of the affected constituencies. Unfortunately, the National Campaign Committee had not discussed the agenda of the meeting with the Regional executives.

Throughout the campaign, one source of constant distraction was the so-called independent groups.

There was the One-touch group, the Friends Of Nana Akufo Addo (FONAA), the Northern Communication Center, a variety of religious groups and a few powerful individuals who just refused to be part of any structure and were still able to get resources to do whatever they wished to do. For example, even though Lawyer Owusu Afriyie had been named as the Regional Communication Director for the campaign, the Northern Communication group was established without the involvement and knowledge of either of us.

These groups competed with the Regional Monitoring Groups for space and influence on the ground. Despite my general disapproval of these groups, one that appeared to be very effective was the Association of Foot Soldiers, formed by Teye Kukrudu, with Ebo Mensah, an assemblyman as the National Co-ordinator. Their events were very well attended and many ordinary party members appreciated their role.

Another factor that led to misunderstanding was defining the role of the Regional Monitoring Teams. The idea was that they were supposed to just monitor and not ran the regional campaigns. This meant that the National Campaign Committee was going to deal with the constituencies directly. In practice, the role of the regional teams depended on their membership and their ability to command resources. In some regions, the original list of the Regional monitors was rejected.

While the Campaign Committee had been inaugurated with a lot of fanfare, some of the team members were never assigned effective roles. Madam Hajia Rukaya and Ms. Mawuse Dake were always complaining about not being kept informed or not getting any roles assigned to them. Hajia Rukaya had a sense of impending doom and was always warning whoever would listen that we were about to go over a cliff.

THE LONG CONVOYS

Throughout the campaign, there were concerns about the length and size of the candidate's convoy. There were repeated attempts to reduce the size of Nana Akufo-Addo's entourage but many were determined to be in the candidate's entourage and would not be deterred. Once, at Akropong, Victor Newman complained about the convoys and was so viciously attacked that one would think he had committed a very serious offense. Indeed, to some, it was not enough to be in the convoy.

They had to be at a particular spot in it and whenever they lost that place they wanted their driver to regain it by any means necessary. One effect of the emphasis on the candidate's campaign was that the whole campaign came to centre on the candidate with harmful consequences. All around the country, regions and constituencies waited to hear that the candidate was coming before they sprang into action. After the candidate's visit, many went back to sleep. Indeed, many Parliamentary candidates, particularly in safe seats, once the primaries were over, did not do much. While there were many big names in the campaign, we never deployed them to effect. It should have been possible to put in the field about six teams, one with the candidate, one with the running mate, one with the President, another with the Vice-President, and others with the wives of the candidate as well as a final one with Alan Kyerematen and say Honourable Osafo Maafo. Despite repeated discussions of these options, there were never put in place.

To this day, many believe that breaking the campaign team up would have been very effective.

These teams would have been more than a match for the NDC trio of teams, led by Professor Mills, former President Rawlings and John Mahama.

Also, it would have energized the party more effectively while reducing the complaints about the lengthy convoys that unfortunately fed the impression that ours was a lavishly financed campaign.

The truth is that while the Presidential candidate and his road team were very hard-working, they just could not do it alone. Nana's team had a lot of energy and our polling showed that whenever they showed up, our numbers improved. The candidate himself, Alan, Osafo Maafo, Kwabena Agyapong and Boakye Agyarko were very good platform speakers and worked very hard. They just could not do it alone.

In retrospect, the Campaign team had virtually all the people who were needed to make our campaign a success. Unfortunately, some were in the wrong roles. Of those in the right roles, their effectiveness was undermined by the existence of too many power centres and the existence of the spending committee which was not accountable to the campaign.

Repeatedly, it was suggested that Jake Obetsebi Lamptey, Dr. Apraku, Peter Mac Manu and Nana Ohene Ntow should be in daily communication for the smooth running of the campaign. Unfortunately, this could not be done. Unfortunately, Dr. Kofi Konadu Apraku and Jake Obetsebi Lamptey until at the very end did not communicate very well despite having offices in the same building. Chairman Peter Mac Manu and the General Secretary Nana Ohene Ntow, due to the problems in their relationship, also did not communicate as much as they should have.

THE UNDER-USED TALENTS

I believe that Jake Obetsebi Lamptey, Dan Botwe, Chairman Mac Manu, Kojo Mpiani and the President, amongst others, were under-utilized.

I have no doubt that involving the Chief of Staff more in the day-to-day running of the campaign would have made it more effective. Between the Chief of Staff, Jake Obetsebi Lamptey and Dan Botwe, there is a lot of the knowledge and experience that won us elections in the past.

Dan Botwe, despite his abrasiveness on occasion, displayed knowledge of electioneering on the ground that was almost unrivalled in the committee. His increased involvement in issues on the ground would have made the campaign more effective. His effectiveness, to be fair, would have been limited by the fact that he was a Parliamentary candidate.

Jake Obetsebi Lamptey's temperament would have been very useful in pulling people together if he had not been marginalized for crucial sections of the campaign.

To be fair to Dr. Apraku, he sometimes had difficulties that, due to the situation he found himself in and his penchant for secrecy limited his effectiveness. I remember the day, during one meeting of the campaign committee when under relentless questioning by Dan Botwe and I, he disclosed that he did not know how much the campaign had raised and spent. As he put it, "As we sit here, they are in Brong-Ahafo. They are spending money so it means someone made a budget. I was not involved at all." The Campaign Committee took it up with the Candidate and that situation was redressed. Also, Dr Apraku seemed to be very prepared for his presentations. For the Campaign strategic plan, his presentation was very detailed and very well put together. Once, I walked into his office and found him very subdued. "You know, this is a very difficult job and I am doing my best. There are things that are simply beyond my control. Most of those complaining about me have no idea how hard this job is", he said.

I never understood why the National Chairman was under-utilized. He has served the party at all levels, from the constituency to the National level and had a very good grasp of how things worked on the ground. However, he seemed unable to exert, either on the campaign or on the party, the natural pull that should have come with his position. He was very involved in training party officials and seemed to be very good at it. In discussions, he was very aware of the lapses but seemed unable to address them. When some say that he was afraid of speaking up, they are wrong. I was at a meeting when Nana said he was not inclined to support public financing of political parties. In response, Mac gave such an impassioned defense of public financing that Nana changed his view on the spot.

THE PRESIDENT

One person who should have been involved more was the President. The question of why and how the President was not more involved will be debated for a long time.

I know for a fact that he assisted the campaign to raise funds. In addition to that, he should have been more involved in reaching out to the public. As late as September 2008, President Kufuor was more popular than either Nana Akufo-Addo or Professor Mills. Getting him to hit the road hard in the last month could certainly have made a difference, in places like Ashanti, Central, Western and Brong-Ahafo regions.

Nana and President Kufuor arrive for Kasoa rally

As earlier referred to, the President, through others, indicated repeatedly that he would "do whatever he is asked to do". I do not know to what extent he was asked or not asked. I am aware that the President and Nana Akufo-Addo had many meetings, sometimes with others and also by themselves. Those meetings were always described by the Presidential candidate as very cordial. Some have stated that in their judgment that the President did not have to be asked to do anything before doing it. As a seasoned political operative, they claim that the President knew whatever needed to be done and could have done it without anybody asking. The question of whether and how he was asked will be discussed in party circles for some time. During the campaign and since, I have spoken to many, some in smaller parties or not directly related to politics, who say they were urged by the President to help the NPP Campaign in many ways. These, together with his strong fund-raising, would suggest strongly that the President was committed to working for our victory. It therefore appears that based on all the evidence available, the view that the President refused to help has no basis in fact. It will be instructive to compare the working relationship between President Kufuor and Nana Akufo-Addo to the one between President Rawlings and Prof. Mills. Historically, such relationships have always been complicated. In 1960, for instance, in the United States, Richard Nixon lost to John Kennedy in one of the closest elections in the last century. In reviewing the elections, many felt that President Eisenhower's lack of full participation in the campaign, may have accounted for the Republicans' defeat. In 2000, when Al Gore lost to George Bush after winning the popular vote, critics blamed Gore for failing to involve Clinton enough.

The Regional Committees also excluded or under-utilized some whose inclusion would have made a positive difference. Just two examples will suffice. In the Ashanti Region, Antoh should have been involved more. His organizational skills are respected across board and his full involvement in the team would have done us a lot of good in the region. Another place where the exclusion of people who were out of favour harmed our chances was the Central Region where Honourable Edumadze, Mr. Kutin and maybe Ms. Christine Churcher would have made the team more effective.

In addition, there were quite a few who despite their obvious talents were over-utilized. For example, despite his obvious talents, it seemed surprising that Honourable Kan Dapaah, who was the full-time Minister of Defence, would have the time to run the most important region in our campaign, Ashanti. A slightly less talented person with a little more time would have been a more appropriate choice for Ashanti Region. During the campaign, the impression was that the teams in Central and Ashanti regions were very hard-working. I was cured of this when I had a chance to visit those regions. In Ashanti, the Campaign Director, Victor Owusu, told me that a month to the election, he had asked for constituency campaign programs and that out of the thirty-nine constituencies, only four had such plans in place. Around the same time, the Regional Organizer, Alhaji Abdullah, informed me that he had no vehicle to travel round the region. In my view, the two people who should have been on the road in the region all the time were Victor and Abdallah. In fact, when Dr Oheneba Owusu Danso joined the campaign for the second round, he too reported that it lacked the crispness and the hunger for victory that was so evident in the 2000 campaign. He reported poor leadership even as a few leaders and many ordinary people struggled to bring the victory that never came. It is a tribute to the region that despite these lapses, they gave us such a lift in the results.

Of course, there were very effective micro-teams in the campaign. The Spending Committee appeared to work very well together. We put on some impressive rallies with Lord Commey at the centre of things. And by the way, it was Lord Commey who suggested the "Kangaroo dance".

So did Gabby Otchere Darko and Dr. Apraku, who got along very well. I worked very well with Jake Obetsebi Lamptey and Dr. Owusu Afriyie Akoto in particular and many others in the campaign. Of those in the regions, Lawyer Owusu Afriyie, alias "Sir John" was a work-horse. He seemed to live at some of the radio stations in Kumasi. With a little more support, he would have been even more effective than he was.

I am sure that some committees, internally worked quite well together. However, given the expertise on the committee and considering how well we got along generally, the Communications Committee would have done wonders if it had had the necessary support to work within its terms of reference. Within days of the inauguration of the Campaign Committee, we had a retreat to map out the outlines of a communication strategy.

NANA AKUFO-ADDO

Throughout the campaign, there was always speculation about how much Nana Akufo-Addo knew about some of the difficulties referred to and when. In the post-election meeting of the Campaign Committee, Nana Akufo-Addo took full responsibility for the failure of the campaign and that was as it should be.

From my observations, it appeared that whenever he had the opportunity to listen to all the necessary parties to a decision, his decisions were timely, to the point and generally excellent.

The question that will be asked for a long time is whether, with the campaign team in place there were enough mechanisms in place to keep the candidate informed about the performance and effectiveness of his team.

Sometimes, it seems, there were advisors who did not serve him well. With unusual access to the candidate, they would get him to make decisions before others with contrary views could make their case and then start implementing the decision with the familiar refrain "Nana Akufo-Addo asked me to do it.", when questioned. Towards the end, one had the feeling that Nana Akufo-Addo had never been asked to authorize many of the decisions he was reported to have authorized. It seemed many of such situations were created by loyal associates, eager to display their influence and no doubt well meaning but afraid of losing influence with the "big man". Of such decisions, the one that comes to mind easily was the decision to have a "BELIEVE IN GHANA" concert. When the plan was announced during a meeting, it was vehemently opposed by Jake Obetsebi Lamptey, Dr. Apraku, Peter Mac Manu and most of those in the room.

When someone said there was a volunteer willing to finance it, Peter Mac Manu exploded "You do not understand. The issue is not whether or not someone is prepared to pay for it. It is whether having the concert is the best use of that money for our campaign." A few days later, the concert came on.

Some have said Nana found it difficult to address issues head on. Not really. He told me directly a number of times that he was receiving complaints that I was "too nice in going after the NDC. I know what you are trying to do but you make too many concessions." Of course I argued back. I explained that in my view, the key constituency was the floating voters and they found my style very effective. One of my proudest days was when I was nominated by him to go onto "GOOD EVENING GHANA" when he was unable to go for a scheduled interview. In the event, METRO decided to cancel the interview. Once, I saw him give one of the key people in the campaign a well-deserved tongue-lashing that would have made any domineering President or leader envious.

One of Nana Akufo-Addo's strengths is that he does not hold grudges. No matter how passionately you argued with him over a point, he never held it against you.

Another very admirable trait Nana Akufo-Addo has is that he is very considerate. During our visit to North America, we were travelling from Toronto to New York when Mustapha Hamid and another member of the team failed to get on the plane because of immigration delays. Nana Akufo-Addo had us wait at JFK airport for two hours while they tried to get a later flight. As he put it "We came together so we must leave together." Earlier in the week, he had held the group back for about ten minutes while he waited for me to finish a conversation after an event.

My best judgment is he found most of the right talent for the campaign but a few were misplaced.

THE "KYEBI MAFIA"

An account of this campaign will be incomplete without any discussion of the so-called "Kyebi Mafia"

First, there were quite a few people in the mafia who did not hail from Kyebi.

Secondly, there were differences within the "mafia". Sometimes, they disagreed amongst themselves as vehemently as they did with outsiders. Sometimes, they undercut one another with a viciousness that they rarely showed to outsiders.

Third, many successful politicians have an inner circle, "kitchen cabinet" or "praetorian guard". To call it a "mafia" makes it sound a little more pejorative and menacing than it was.

The idea of an inner circle has always existed in politics. It is reported that President Kennedy, who was always accused of being surrounded by an "Irish mafia" once asked someone who was not Irish to serve in his cabinet and the person said "no". When the President-elect asked why, the guy said "because the Irish-mafia around you will eat me alive." The President smiled. "Do you know why I want you to join my administration?" "No sir," he replied. "Well" said the President, "to protect me from them".

It is very impressive that Nana Akufo-Addo has a large family and associates who are all so eager to help him realize his political ambitions. They should be commended for their interest in him and in politics. It is obvious that many in his family have very impressive credentials and talents. The likes of Ken Ofori-Atta and Nana Bediatuo, to mention just a few are very gifted. Indeed, it will be tragic to deprive him of such talent because it comes from his family. Just as Dr. Kwame Addo Kufuor was such an undoubted asset to his brother, President Kufuor, those with the requisite skills and talents must be encouraged to assist Nana Akufo-Addo. During the campaign, Ken Ofori-Atta, to me was a very good sounding board and channel to pass information to the candidate. And so was Edward Akufo-Addo, known to many as BUMPTY.

I found that when the "family" was unhappy with me about one thing or the other, Nana Ofori-Atta was very good at relaying to me the concerns and taking back my perspectives. He was a very honest and reliable person to deal with.

Some members of the family are exceptionally hardworking; Gabby Otchere Darko for instance, was one of the hardest-working and gifted people I met in the campaign but he was sometimes very difficult to get along with. He put in incredible hours towards the success of the campaign. He offended people with casual abandon and seemed to rub many people the wrong way. On the other hand, he was very loyal to people and to his staff.

I have no doubt that the family has the best intentions in whatever they do. However, sometimes, in their eagerness to serve Nana's interest, they ruffle feathers, sometimes very badly and gratuitously.

Sometimes, in the case of some of them, their eagerness is not always matched by tact and skill. Some of them have harmed his reputation with careless talk, about his intentions and about others.

It appears to me that the "mafia" must find a balance where their undoubted strengths can serve Nana Akufo-Addo without alienating people unnecessarily. There are some in that family whose talents, significant as they are, would be better if deployed outside the public spotlight. Also, despite their undoubted abilities, they are , sometimes, too eager to cater to his whims rather than to set him straight. They must learn that the ultimate task of a political team is to make their principal more effective.

If they really care about him, as much as I presume they do, they would adjust their behavior accordingly, to make themselves and Nana Akufo-Addo more effective. It is surprising how often people say "The problem is not him. It is those over-educated, over-westernised, spoiled and arrogant Kyebi guys around him". And by the way, some of the women in that family turn people off more than any of the men.

Of course, the deployment of personnel is always the prerogative of a candidate. It is up to Nana Akufo-Addo to learn the strengths and weaknesses of those who desire to serve him and to deploy them to his best advantage. As many politicians have learnt painfully, it pays, sometimes, to put competence ahead of loyalty and those who succeed, do this routinely. Ultimately, success in politics requires a judicious mixture of talent, loyalty and skilled team-building. To get to the Presidency, Nana must reach significantly beyond his family. I have no doubt that in the end, he will do whatever is necessary. Once, I was there when he addressed a complaint that one of the "mafia" had said something uncomplimentary about a very prominent politician. After berating the person for showing such bad judgement, he said wearily "You know whenever you do things like this, they blame me".

CHAPTER SIX
CHOOSING THE RUNNING MATE

"I don't care how good he is. All I want to know is whether he is lucky. With luck, one can achieve a lot in life."

- Napoleon Bonaparte.

PREVIOUS RUNNING MATES

HISTORICALLY, OUR PARTY HAS ALWAYS HAD a difficult time choosing running mates. Even when Victor Owusu, our Presidential candidate for 1979 election picked the Tolon-Na, Alhaji Yakubu Tali, who was generally very well regarded in the party, there were grumblings. It is reported that Victor had gone to congress with Madjitey high on his list but when the Tolon-Na put in a strong performance, Victor had to change plans and pick him. Those days, the running mate was announced almost immediately after the candidate was picked. Later, Victor had to send Appiah-Menka to pacify Madjitey.

Professor Adu Boahen's choice of Roland Alhassan in 1992 was well-received. This was for two reasons. First, Adu Boahen's hold on the party was almost unchallenged. Second, Mr. Alhassan was considered a party heavyweight in his own right.

When President Kufuor picked Alhaji Aliu Mahama for the 2000 election, there was a near-rebellion. When Aliu was announced at a National Executive meeting in Ho, it was greeted by deafening silence. Then people erupted in protests. A few choice words were exchanged between President Kufuor and one or two others at the meeting. Quite a few of our prominent members walked out of the meeting in disgust. It is alleged that quite a few people believed they had been promised the running mate slot by Mr. Kufuor. Amongst these were Prof. Wayo Seini and late Madam Rebecca Hawa Yakubu. Of course, Mr. Kufuor and his team denied this. One person who was actually offered the number two slot of the 2000 ticket and turned it down was Dr. Edward Mahama of the P.N.C. To return to the 2000 running mate issue, with just a little time left for the party to announce the running-mate, there was little that could be done. As Elizabeth Ohene recalls, " General Secretary Dan Botwe went out to the assembled press and did a masterful job extolling the virtues of Alhaji Aliu Mahama. That day, Dan Botwe truly rose in my estimation."

The next morning, according to Ms. Ohene, Mr Kufuor summoned his embattled running-mate, gave him a long list of party elders and ordered him to get to work selling himself to them. To be fair to Alhaji Mahama, despite the disquiet that greeted his nomination, he had been a stalwart of the party for some time. According to the Party Administrator, Mr. Antwi-Agyei, when Mr Da Rocha dispatched former General Secretary Agyenim Boateng and him to the north in 1991 to quietly rouse the party in anticipation that the ban on politics would be lifted, it was Alhaji Aliu Mahama who met them, arranged for their accommodation and bore most of their expenses regarding the trip. Reportedly, he quietly supported the party financially throughout the nineties.

RUNNING FOR RUNNING-MATE

For the 2008 elections, the search for a running mate got underway long before the primaries were over. There were rumours of who would be whose running-mate even during the primary.

Was it going to be a North-South ticket, a South-North ticket or a South-South ticket? In the north, where Vice-President Aliu Mahama was trying to rally people around his banner, it was rumoured that some opposed his bid because it would doom their chances of becoming running mates. This was to have long-term ramifications during our Parliamentary primary elections.

Across the party, there were whispered conversations about going South-South this time while others still held to the traditional North-South idea.

Even though President Rawlings had won the north twice decisively without a northerner on his ticket, our party traditionalists were convinced that we could never win with a South-south ticket.

Indeed, before the choice of our running mate for the 2008 elections, internal polling showed clearly that large majorities of the north, of the south and of women did not care where the running mate came from as long as he/she was deemed competent.

With so many aspirants and the chance of a second round, the running mate issue was dangled before quite a few people in creative ways to turn their minds by all the leading candidates.

The dust had hardly settled at Legon when the lobbying got underway. Whereas in the past, lobbying to be running mate had been done discreetly, this time, it became a full-blown public campaign with spokespersons and public displays. In this case, the battle was for the vote of one man, Nana Akufo-Addo.

The front-runners were Hajia Alima Mahama, Alhaji Siddique Boniface, Alhaji Malik Yakubu, Alhaji Mustapha Iddris and some long-shot southerners. The most frequently mentioned southerners were Madam Oboshie Sai, Jake Obetsebi-Lamptey and less frequently, Alan Kyerematen. Later, Rashid Bawa was added to the mix.

Indeed, when Nana Akufo-Addo met the former aspirants one-on-one, he told me that he had three names he was considering for running mate: Hajia Alima Mahama, Alhaji Mustapha Idris and Alhaji Malik Alhassan. He explained that he had briefly contemplated a South-South ticket but felt it would be best to stick with the traditional north-south ticket. He said that he knew all three of them very well and would not have trouble working with any of them. He asked for my view of all three and I gave it. I am told that he asked other aspirants of their views as well and they gave it.

NPP vice-presidential aspirants

Unknown to many, the candidate had also decided that he did not want to determine his succession and would therefore not pick any of those who contested him since they were likely to run again. According to Osafo Maafo, he did not want "to give anyone an advantage in 2016".

Soon after the primary, delegations from the north came to see him to press the case for the north in general and for particular candidates, repeatedly.

Right after the primary, I gave Nana Akufo-Addo a confidential memorandum about the process for picking a running mate.

During a campaign committee meeting in June, he announced that he had been thinking over the issue regarding his running mate and said he would assemble a search committee to identify and submit the names of potential nominees. He also indicated that he wanted a running mate from the north.

Once the candidate made it clear that he wanted a running mate from the North, there was a lot of ethnic politics. Of course, when the candidate said "north", he meant the three northern regions, not just the northern region.

The Dagombas have the numbers as far as the north is concerned. Therefore, whenever there is talk about having a running-mate from the north, that talk starts with them. Many felt that if our running mate was going to be a Dagomba, that person should not be linked to the Dagbon crisis. However, from the Dagombas, the prime candidates were Alhaji Malik Yakubu and Alhaji Mustapha Idris.

The next group to consider were the Gonjas. The key people here were Ahaji Siddique Boniface and the Lepo-Wura, Alhaji Jawula. At the eleventh hour, Adam Zachariah, Principal of Gabagaba Training College came into the picture and seemed to be quite popular.

Hajia Alima Mahama is a Mamprusi. Some said the ramifications of her nomination would be felt as far as Bawku because of the Bawku crisis involving the Mamprusis and the Kusasis. In reality, the effects of any nomination is felt all over the country. I remember receiving a call from Dr. Kwaku Afriyie, the former Minister of Health and the NPP Parliamentary candidate for Sefwi-Wiawso. He argued very persuasively that in addition to considering which group a nominee attracts, we should also look at which group that nominee repels. He pointed out that in his constituency, there were a lot of Kusasis who would not be pleased by a Mamprusi nominee unless that nominee was packaged very carefully.

There was, of course the angle of religion and how the nominee's religion would affect the vote.

Unknown to many in the party, there had been a couple of little-known incidents during the primaries, which would cast a long shadow over the search for a running-mate.

When the issue climaxed, some in the party began blaming Mustapha Hamid for using his influence to foist Hajia Alima Mahama on Nana Akufo-Addo. Mustapha in turn revealed that during the campaign for the party's flag bearer slot, Nana Akufo-Addo had pledged to Hajia's constituents at Walewale that if elected, he would make her his running mate. According to Mustapha, while interpreting what Nana Akufo-Addo was saying, he paused to seek confirmation before interpreting it to the audience.

The Presidential candidate, Nana Akufo-Addo, indeed confirmed that he planned to make Hajia his running-mate. Later on, he repeated this pledge to Hajia who naturally, passed on the good news to others to spread.

Nana Akufo-Addo, it appeared, was determined to live up to the pledge he had made to the people of Walewale.

Then there was Boniface Abubakar Saddique. While he did a very good job with the media and with the public, he forgot to woo the candidate and so as things went to their dramatic climax, in the candidate's mind, he was never in contention for the slot. Apparently, right after the nomination, Nana Akufo-Addo sent him a caution to cease making the issue of a running-mate a public spectacle. Boniface, it appeared, chose to ignore the counsel from the man whose running-mate he hoped to be. The presence of Alhaji Jawula in the running-mate chase led to an incident where Alhaji Jawula, a civil servant was spotted at a rally with an NPP "T-SHIRT". Eventually, he resigned as a civil servant. Another dramatic incident occurred in Salaga when during a rally, the Overlord of Gonjaland, the Yagbonwura, Bawa Doshie,, pointedly told the candidate in public that the people of Salaga would prefer Alhaji Jawula as running-mate. While the traditional ruler should not have given his advise in public, Boniface made a bad situation worse by complaining about his chief's comment in public. In a profession defined mainly by ambition, Boniface was considered by many close to the candidate as "too ambitious" and a man who would stop at nothing to be Vice-President on his way to the Presidency.

HOW HAJIA WAS UNDONE

With a few weeks to go for the deadline, on the 3rd of July, people around the candidate decided to try a selective leak to test the public's reaction. They planted a story on the front-page of the "DAILY GRAPHIC" that disclosed that Hajia Alima Mahama was the front-runner in the race to be Nana Akufo-Addo's running mate. The story, on the front-page of the "DAILY GRAPHIC" quoted sources close to the candidate as indicating that "the three comprised two men and a woman, who appeared to be the frontrunner". The story identified the three as Minister for Works and Housing, Alhaji Abubakar Siddique Boniface, the Chief Director of the Ministry of Health, Lepowura Alhaji Mohammed Nuru Deen Jawula and the Minister for Women's and Children's' Affairs Hajia Alima Mahama. When reached by the "GRAPHIC" Hajia said "As a true-blue member of the NPP who had been part of its struggles from the days in opposition, she had the requisite experience and competence, to handle the job of Vice-President of the Republic of Ghana."

The story was given more credence by the fact that a few weeks before, the paper had successfully predicted that John Mahama would be the NDC running-mate.

With this publication, the race erupted with new intensity onto the newspaper front-pages and radio talk-shows. In addition people started sending text messages about the candidates, most of which were negative. A few days after the "DAILY GRAPHIC" publication, I was in Tamale with Gabby Otchere Darko when the issue came up during discussions with a cross-section of party members. "Oh, it is going to be Hajia. The decision has already been made", Gabby said without any hesitation in his voice. There was stunned silence that seemed to last a long time. Then someone changed the topic.

Suddenly, those opposing the nomination had a new sense of urgency. Some went to Nana to urge him, "not to do this to the party". Others went to party leaders and elders to make the case against Hajia. Traditional rulers, many from the north, started reaching out to party leaders to help change the candidate's mind. Amongst those who were contacted were Ama Busia, Appiah Menkah and Da Rocha.

The crux of the argument against Hajia was that while she was a fine lady, it would be difficult, particularly in the north to sell an unmarried woman on the ticket.

Her supporters argued that the opposition to her nomination was sexist and that her life story as a poor girl who managed to become a lawyer and a single woman raising a child by herself would inspire many women. Unfortunately, many and probably a majority of those opposed to her were women.

Then da Rocha spoke. He said choosing Hajia would be a mistake and that if the candidate insisted on picking her, the party should be prepared to change the candidate.

In an emergency meeting, some suggested that the Campaign Committee should attack Da Rocha while others suggested that it would be suicidal to do so since many in the party shared his sentiments. In the end, a statement was issued, under my signature, praising da Rocha for his service to the party and pointing out that the candidate had not chosen a running-mate yet. With that, Hajia's candidature was over. The day before this, I received a text message from one of Nana's advisors which read in part "Nana has stood by you despite attacks by Alan and others and you should stand by him on this issue. It has been hard to involve you in this selection because we were never sure where you stood."

BAWUMIA EMERGES

Theoretically, that would have left Alhaji Saddique Boniface, and the Lepowura, Mohammed Nuru Deen Jawula. For the candidate, however, with Hajia out, he needed a new candidate..

Over the next few days, two new candidates emerged, Adam Zachariah, Principal of Bagabaga, Training College and the Chair of the Northern Region Finance Committee of the NPP and Dr. Mamudu Bawumia, Deputy Governor of the Bank of Ghana.

Two days before the National Executive meeting scheduled to discuss it, Gabby Otchere Darko called me. "Yesterday, Nana had a very good meeting with Adam Zachariah so he will be okay. He is still going to talk to Dr. Bawumia too and then we will see."

The next day, Gabby called again. "It is going to be Bawumia".

That afternoon, Gabby and I visited Dr. Bawumia. He seemed surprised by all that was happening but he carried himself very well. I was concerned by his admission that he had never been a party member.

The next morning, on Joy FM, I defended the process for selecting the running-mate. I said that either Hajia Alima or Dr. Bawumia would be excellent candidates. While some felt I had not been aggressive enough in promoting Bawumia, I was worried about going out on a limb when so much seemed to be influx.

Throughout the process, I had been in constant communication with Ken Ofori-Atta and Bumpty. Ken and his wife were very much in favour of Hajia. Ken's wife, Angie, was very eloquent in defense of Hajia and her candidacy. She felt it would be a great thing for the cause of women and that while she was happily married, she felt it was sexist for people to use against Hajia the fact that she was not married.

Bumpty, while not against Hajia, was concerned about the resistance her candidacy was facing all across the party and worked behind the scenes to make sure his brother made the right decision.

The night before the announcement of the running-mate, I reached Ken Ofori-Atta. I told him that many in the party were concerned about the fact that Dr. Bawumia was not a member of the party, stating that while the antipathy was not as pronounced as that concerning Hajia, it was there and needed to be dealt with.

It was probably the only time Ken sounded angry in all the time I dealt with him in the campaign.

"What is the poor guy supposed to do? He picks Hajia and people say "no". He picks Bawumia and despite excitement all around the country, people say "no" again. Did President Kufuor not get Aliu? Why did everybody accept Aliu? Why are we treating Nana Akufo-Addo differently from JAK?"

On the morning the nomination was to be announced, a Campaign Committee meeting was scheduled to discuss the choice with the candidate. When I got to the campaign office, I learned that the meeting had been cancelled.

I had spoken to Jake Obetsebi Lamptey earlier that morning and called him to ask why he had not told me about the cancellation. He expressed surprise about the fact that the meeting had been cancelled and said that he had not been informed.

Over the airwaves, it was beginning to leak that it would be Dr. Bawumia and some in the party, including Honourable Kennedy Agyapong were vowing resistance. He condemned the proposed choice and said if Dr. Bawumia was picked, he would leave them to campaign alone. When I was scheduled to respond, some in the campaign urged me to go after him but I refused. I said while I disagreed with his style of expressing himself, he was a very respected party member and that I was confident that when the decision was made, Honourable Kennedy Agyapong would support it fully.

The National Executive Committee meeting was attended by the President, Vice-President and many party elders. After disposing of other issues, Nana Akufo-Addo got up to present his nominee.

He said it had been a difficult decision. First, he had been very interested in picking Hajia but it appeared there was a lot of resistance to that choice by the party.

Then there was Malik who was perhaps best qualified and his personal preference but his choice was made impossible by his implication in the Dagbon crisis.

Therefore, he had settled on Dr. Mamudu Bawumia. He acknowledged that while Dr. Bawumia had no association with our party, his father had had a rather complicated association with the Danquah-Busia tradition. He pleaded, however, that "we should not visit the sins of the father upon the son".

It was a short but very effective speech.

The discussions that followed made me proud as a party member. It was principled and serious. There were strenuous objections to Dr. Bawumia's nomination by Ama Busia, Harona Esseku, Dan Botwe, Papa Owusu Ankomah, Kwabena Agyapong and myself. Ama Busia was particularly eloquent on that side. She was very passionate, very well-informed and very eloquent. At one point, looking the candidate straight in the eye, she said, "It is very appropriate that the candidate has wisely asked that we should not visit the sins of the father upon the son. Otherwise, I would have a lot to say about what the father did to harm the Danquah-Busia tradition."

The group supporting the nomination were led by the President and included Osafo Maafo, Mike Ocquaye, Bin Salia and the Vice-President. On that side, the Vice-President was the most eloquent. The President's comments were also very helpful to the nomination.

The Vice-President said that he had also faced the same issues when he was nominated and had been able to overcome his obstacles. He pledged to "hold the hand of Dr. Bawumia and help him to succeed".

When the issue of Dr. Bawumia's membership of the party was raised, Dr. Apraku said he had been informed that Dr. Bawumia had a card. The President cut him off."We are all politicians and we know what is happening so let us not go there."

In the end, as Dan Botwe put it, "once Nana Akufo-Addo proposed Dr. Bawumia, he was as good as nominated".

The NPP constitution requires the Presidential candidate to nominate his running mate in consultation with the National Executive Committee. The question was the meaning of "consult". As someone suggested, just being informed could be interpreted as consultation.

A few days afterwards, I met Prof. Oquaye who tried to put it all in perspective. He said it was God who picked leaders and that his ways were not the ways of the world. He urged understanding for Nana Akufo-Addo because he needed someone he could work comfortably with and that Dr. Bawumia would make a good complement to the flag bearer.

In response, I said "I understand all that but many are confused about the commitment to principles of our party. We disqualified many good party members from contesting as Parliamentary candidates because "they had not nurtured the party enough". How then could we pick as Vice-President, one whose member ship of the party was even questionable? Tomorrow, if the National Chairman met any of those he had disqualified on grounds of not nurturing the party, would he apologize to that party member for his disqualification?"

With that, Dr. Bawumia became the NPP nominee for the Vice-Presidency.

In picking a Vice-President, one is picking someone, either for his electoral assets or for his/her governing assets. A governing choice is one who would not help you win but once in office, will be an asset.

In picking Dick Cheney, President Bush made a governing choice and almost paid for that at the polls. Many felt there were others who could have brought particular states into the Republican column. Once Mr. Bush was elected, however, most Americans were re-assured to have the very experienced Mr. Cheney by his side. As the world and Ghana faced economic challenges, there is no doubt that Dr. Bawumia would have been an undoubted asset as Vice-President of Ghana. Therefore, his choice could be described as a bold governing choice by Nana Akufo-Addo.

BAWUMIA ON THE CAMPAIGN TRAIL

In the end, it appears that John Mahama brought more to the NDC ticket than Dr. Bawumia brought to the NPP ticket. When Dr. Bawumia went to visit the press after his nomination, he was going to introduce himself, but when John Mahama went, he was visiting old friends.

While towards the end, Dr. Bawumia took off on his own to campaign and worked very hard, he never had the impact that John Mahama had.

Right from the beginning, not enough thought went into choosing his entourage. Given his relative inexperience, he should have been surrounded by more seasoned people from the party. The people around him were new and most were as inexperienced as he was and this did not help. With the exception of John Boadu, none of the entourage knew the party well. Surrounding him with the likes first Vice-Chairman Alhaji Musah, Campaign Committee member Hajia Rukaya, National Women's Organizer Rita Asobayire and others would have made him more effective.

Ironically, even when we had our "Manifesto launch", Dr Bawumia was not put on stage to explain our economic policies. While politically, he did not bring as much to our ticket, we may not have played to his strengths. One asset he brought, though, was his wife, Samira. She was effective on the platform and very well liked. She and Mrs. Akufo-Addo were very well-liked and could have been very effective, particularly in Greater Accra.

While Dr. Bawumia is a fine man and would have been an asset in government, maybe his choice was a reach too far. That is why we suffered losses even in the Mamprusi area where he hails from.

Next time, we will do well to heed the advice President H. W. Bush is reported to have given his son George W. Bush about picking a running mate based on his experience after picking Senator Dan Quayle as his running-mate in 1988. Dan Quayle, even though a Senator, was seen as an unsuccessful Vice-President. In advising his son George W. Bush, the elder President Bush said "Son" he said "Pick a solid, well-known party person".

CHAPTER SEVEN
THE MANIFESTO

" Words without deeds are nothing."

David Ben Gurion, first Prime Minister of Israel

THE MANIFESTO COMMITTEE HAD THE FIRST Committee meeting of the campaign, before the inauguration of the Campaign Committee. At that meeting, Dr. Owusu Afriyie Akoto , the convener, announced that he had been tasked by Nana Akufo-Addo to co-ordinate the activities of the Manifesto Committee. He revealed that during the presidential primaries, Nana Akufo-Addo's team had developed a manifesto and that he had been tasked to expand that manifesto to include the key ideas of all the other presidential aspirants. To this end, he asked the aspirants to deliver as soon as possible to him, any documents they had developed during the primaries and also provide names of their team members who wished to participate in the development of the manifesto join the effort.

Subsequently, Dr. Afriyie Akoto was confirmed as Chair of the Manifesto Committee. The committee had a very large membership and soon broke up into sub-groups. Amongst these were the Economic, Health and Social Services, Infrastructure and various other sub-groups.

It was agreed that each sub-group would develop its proposals and that afterwards, the committee as a whole would meet to debate particular reports from particular committees. In the event, most of the sub-committees never convened. Instead, assisted by a few trusted people, Dr. Afriyie tried to comb through the many documents submitted and tried to merge the various inputs. Amongst those who were most interested in the work of the committee were Boakye-Agyarko, Yoofi Grant and Freda Prempeh.

When the first drafts started circulating, it turned out that quite a few Ministers had concerns that they had not had a chance to give input. As a result, during the National Executive Committee meeting that discussed the nomination of Dr. Bawumia, the President proposed a joint meeting between the Campaign Committee and the government to exchange information and to fully inform those developing our manifesto.

During the meeting, held at Akosombo, many Ministers made presentations on the achievements of the government. The late Kwadwo Baah Wiredu, Felix Owusu Agyapong and Joe Ghartey were very active during the meeting. The Vice-President and the Chief of Staff were both in attendance and very active.

After the meeting, Dr. Afriyie Akoto and Prof. Mike Ocquaye got to work to assemble the data.

IDEAS FOR SPEECHES

Despite this effort, whenever there was going to be a major speech, the Campaign Director would convene a "Committee of Experts" to discuss the substantive outline of the speech. Most of these ideas were from the "Manifesto" but were enriched by the discussions. These meetings were intellectually very stimulating. It was a joy to hear the exchanges between Alan Kyerematen, Dr. Apraku, Osafo Maafo, Boakye-Agyarko and Ahomka-Lindsay, amongst others. Once these outlines were developed and turned into speeches, they became the definitive word on the manifesto. Virtually all these meetings were attended by the candidate and the other participants varied from topic to topic. Initially Korantemaa Adi Dako acted as the editor for speeches and was good to work with.

With regards to healthcare, after an agreement with Dr. Afriyie Akoto, who coordinated development of the Manifesto, I worked with Honourable Abraham Dwumah Odum, Deputy Minister for Health to convene a team of health professionals in Kumasi one week-end. After two days, we produced a seven page paper that survived virtually intact into the manifesto. Later in the campaign, for the candidate's major speech on Healthcare, I relied on the outline developed in Kumasi to write the first draft and then discussed the draft with Professor Frimpong Boateng as well as Dr Opoku Adusei of the Ghana Medical Association, who both made very useful suggestions to improve the speech.

For both the AGI and the IEA speeches, all the big names were there. Many added very good ideas to the speeches but my repeated protests that the speeches were getting too long fell on deaf ears.

The Northern Development Authority speech was also very interesting. Even though many Northerners were summoned including some Vice-Presidential aspirants, in the end, my main collaborator was Ken Ofori-Atta. He assembled an impressive array of data to help make the case for the under-development of the North and brought many ideas to the table on how to develop the North. He demonstrated an interest in the North that was pleasantly surprising. To my surprise, after the first meeting, many of the Northerners did not show much interest.

Our campaign was a little displeased with the conduct of the UDS authorities. I was there when Dr. Apraku met the UDS Vice-Chancellor to discuss whether UDS could host the event that had been in planning for months. Surprisingly, the UDS authorities started claiming that the whole thing was an initiative by the University and that they planned to organize similar events for other candidates.

On the morning of the speech, when I got to Tamale, I discovered that the twelve-page draft I submitted had ballooned to twenty-eight pages. As Nana left for the day's campaigning, he said to me "See what you can do. I am counting on you." During the day, he kept calling with more ideas. Despite this, with the assistance of Irene, Nana's Secretary, I managed to get it down to twenty-one pages. It was very well-delivered and very well received.

MANIFESTO LAUNCH

The week-end before the launch of our manifesto, I received a call that it had been scheduled for Kumasi. Some on the Communication team tried to have the launch done in Accra but were unsuccessful.

There were also concerns about some of those scheduled to speak at the launch. It was suggested that the running mate, who was an economist should be involved in discussing the section on the economy while someone with more expertise in health and/or education should have done the sections relating to them, rather Mustapha Hamid, who did those sections. After all, the central themes of our campaign were supposed to be health and education. Hamid did a good job during his presentation. In the end, we ended up cutting the launch short because there was too much noise in the arena at the Cultural Centre and many in attendance were finding it difficult to follow the language. One very regrettable omission during the launch was our failure to thank the Institute of Economic Affairs (I.E.A.) for their Financial Support in preparing the manifesto.

During the early part of the function, since I was circulating in the crowd, I realized many in the crowd were not following the presentations because it was in English. When I suggested that presenters mix in a little bit of Twi, it was rejected. However, when Alan realized the crowd was inattentive and started speaking Twi, the crowd became attentive immediately.

In the end, while this was the best manifesto ever prepared by our party, the language and the relative lengths did not demonstrate the relative importance of the various parts to us. It was not possible to look at the manifesto and tell from it that healthcare, for instance, mattered more to us than culture.

To some extent, we tried to address this with a shorter version of the manifesto but it was not marketed well.

On the stump, people complained that we never got the balance right between defending our record and laying out our vision right. Repeatedly, we were accused of spending too much time in defence of our record as opposed to laying out our vision. In the manifesto though, the relative lengths were right.

Despite agreement in principle to do so, we were also never able to designate spokespersons for the various sections of the manifesto. The result was that there was a lot of variation in our presentations on the manifesto.

The week-end after it was launched, our regional communicators were invited to Accra to discuss the manifesto and how to lay it out.

Yoofi Grant, Gabby Otchere Darko and I took turns discussing various aspects of the manifesto. Towards the end, I started asking mock questions and most of the responses were not good. Kwamena Duncan and about two others were, however, very succinct. It became apparent that we had a lot of work to do, with the others. Generally, we tended to focus on the national stations and newspapers but beyond these, there were many other stations and media markets that people listened to. An example of this was Kumasi. Morning hosts like Kwame Adinkra of ANGEL FM are just as important as any of the big hosts in Accra. While the importance of Kumasi was never in dispute, we never got Sir John the assistance he needed to do effective co-ordination of our efforts in the region. To be sure, there were a lot of people who if marshaled correctly, could have done a marvelous job for us. Many of these were Members of Parliament or MP's but given our inability to tailor campaign priorities to spending, we were always playing catch-up with the NDC.

NDC PROPAGANDA

Some have said it is no accident that while the NDC had a full-time propaganda Secretary in the person of Fiifi Kwetey, the NPP did not find it necessary to fill the position of Communication Director till after the Election. Actually, in the past, the NPP had a Director of Communication in the person of Adu Kwabena Essem, a seasoned journalist. He was relieved of the position in 2005 by the Ohene Ntow administration. After letting the Director go, the leadership could not agree on a replacement till after the election. Of course, in addition to that, we also failed to appoint a Director for Election Strategy.

When the NDC started their propaganda, everybody agreed that it needed to be countered. Indeed, in the retreat done right after the Communication Committee was inaugurated, the importance of propaganda was duly recognized. The NDC Press Conferences, called "SETTING THE RECORD STRAIGHT" had nothing to do with truth. It should have been called "PEDDLING LIES". They told lies about drugs, violence and corruption repeatedly and linked these lies to our candidate, our government and our party. Nobody recognized this better than the candidate."Kennedy, what are we going to do about these?" he asked. However, the budget prepared upon request by the candidate to fund putting out the truth on the NDC falsehoods and doing some propaganda on our own was not funded by the campaign. After some time, with help from Hon. Asamoah Boateng, we started doing some Press Conferences of our own. In the last two months, we finally had some resources to start countering the NDC falsehoods but we had left it quite late. We did some very good work with the help of Sammy Crabbe of Greater Accra, Kwadwo Owusu Afriyie of Ashanti, Adu Gyan of Brong-Ahafo, Kwamena Duncan of Central Region and Clifford Braimah of Northern Region.

PREBUTTING THE NDC MANIFESTO

One bright spot on the manifestoes was when we got an advance copy of the NDC manifesto and wrote a rebuttal statement ahead of their manifesto launch. Working with Gabby, I put out a carefully worded statement pointing out the falsehoods in the statements of Professor Mills, President Rawlings and Chairman Dr. Kwabena Adjei in their introductory statements.. We pointed out factual errors in Prof Mills statements on education, Guineaworm and jobs, amongst others. It was very well-received and knocked them off their stride considerably.

The problems with the manifesto were highlighted by a call that I received from Bumpty a few days after the NDC manifesto. He said he had been told that the NDC manifesto had been on the internet within four hours while ours had taken over four days to get on line. This had resulted from farming out sections of our work without central co-ordination. Earlier in the campaign, I had contacted the person who had designed my web-site for the Presidential primaries and he had agreed to design web-sites for the party and the campaign at cost. However, it was not possible for us to effectively come to terms and work out details with him.

At one point, upon instructions from my committee, I negotiated advertising on "GHANAWEB" through their local agent, Adwoa Agyekum, for the duration of the campaign and submitted the document for approval. I was told that someone else had indicated that he could get a better rate from "GHANAWEB". As a result, we never advertised on "GHANAWEB".

In the end, we had a very good manifesto that we did not sell well. Once we got the message, the candidate stuck to the message of the manifesto, pounding the themes of education, healthcare and jobs relentlessly. Other speakers were not so disciplined and we could never agree on designated spokespersons for various topics.

CHAPTER EIGHT
STRATEGY

"Make no little plans, they have no magic to stir men's blood and probably themselves will not be realized. Make big plans, aim high in hope and work, remembering that a noble, logical diagram, one recorded, will never die."

Daniel Burnham

THE QUESTION OF WHAT WAS GOING to be our fundamental approach to the election was not clear until June 2008. Till then, the candidate had spent time visiting the Constituencies we lost and generally touting the NPP's economic record.

While we were putting together our strategy, Greater-Accra, unbeknown to most of us, had developed a very comprehensive plan for their Region through some strategic planning retreats. These retreats were organized by the Regional Executives led by Sammy Crabbe and facilitated by Roger Koranteng of GIMPA. In their strategic plan they had targeted winning 60% of the votes in Greater-Accra. It turns out that their budget for winning 60% of the votes in Greater-Accra was less than the campaign spent in our losing effort.

Then in the first week of July, I got a call from Ken Ofori-Atta to meet Larry Gibson. Mr. Gibson, I was told, was an African-American law professor in Maryland who doubled as a political strategist. As he later told me, he had helped elect Eileen Johnson Sirleaf of Liberia and Marc Ravelomana of Madagascar. He had also been involved in campaigns Latin America.

During our meeting, Larry Gibsom revealed that he had with the agreement of the candidate, commissioned a baseline poll on the 2008 elections and also reviewed the AFROBAROMETER poll.

After he shared his perspectives with me and four or so others who were present, he indicated that he had met the candidate and some other key people in the campaign to share his perspectives. In response to my questions he indicated that he had not met either Dr. Apraku or the National Chairman. I arranged for them to meet immediately and also suggested that he should meet the key people in the campaign as a group, rather than meeting them individually or in small groups to present his findings. I felt it was important for the campaign to formally evaluate his information and to make decisions on them as a group.

When we met, he presented his findings to the group with his recommendations. Those present with me included Jake Obetsebi Lamptey, Ken Ofori-Atta, Gabby Otchere Darko, Angie Ofori-Atta, Geddy Laryea and Oboshie Sai-Coffie. Also briefed separately, I am told were the National Chairman, Dan Botwe and the candidate.

He asked us all three basic questions:

First, he wanted to know our opinions on who would win if Presidents Rawlings and Kufuor were the respective candidates of their parties.

Most of us felt Kufuor would win but he said that he had done an unscientific survey with 6 respondents who described themselves as independents on the same issue and that 4 of them felt President

Rawlings would win. He said that should tell us about how people on the streets saw things compared to us.

Then he asked us to imagine December 8th. :

"If you lose, why would you have lost?" he asked.

The third was "If you win, why would you have won?"

Later, in conversation, Larry told me he had informed Nana Akufo-Addo in one of their early meetings that he was waiting for the completion of a survey that would measure his favourability and disapproval ratings against that of Professor Mills. According to Larry he then asked Nana Akufo-Addo who he thought would be more popular. Nana Akufo-Addo, according to Larry felt he would be more popular than Professor Mills. When the results came in, Professor Mills was slightly more popular that Nana Akufo-Addo. However, the NPP was more popular than the NDC.

Reviewing the polls, he indicated that Nana Akufo-Addo would win the first round but would not get an outright majority and that the second round would be too close to call. There were 27% of the voters who claimed to be undecided. Later, Larry started referring to them as "UNDECLARED" rather than "UNCOMMITTED". However, when pressed further, he said he would give the second round to Prof. Mills by a whisker.

On support, he indicated that we were strong in Ashanti, Eastern and Brong Ahafo and nearly even in the north but were not doing well at all in Volta, Central and Greater-Accra.

He indicated that we should write off the Central and Greater Accra regions. On this, virtually the entire group disagreed with him. We all agreed that conceding those regions would be tantamount to conceding defeat in the elections.

KEY CAMPAIGN MESSAGES

Mr. Gibson's most surprising recommendation, however, was on the key messages for the campaign. He said across the country, the NPP administration was receiving strong approval for its performance in healthcare, education, infrastructure and freedoms. On the other hand, we were receiving very strong disapproval on corruption, jobs and the economy.

On hearing this, the leadership of the Campaign found this very difficult to accept. We all believed the NPP had given Ghana its best economy in our post-independence history. Therefore, we could not accept that the economy could be a liability.

Larry clinched the argument by saying "Well, it is up to you guys but here is how things look. The people of Ghana think you have done an excellent job on healthcare and education and a very good job on infrastructure and freedoms. You can choose to argue with them on whether their economic circumstances have improved or not but you will lose that argument. On the other hand, you can agree with them that you have given them good healthcare and education and promise them more of that. I think that is the path to victory." After a contentious debate, the team accepted his recommendation.

However, with time, it seemed that not everyone accepted the recommendations wholeheartedly. We kept returning to that argument throughout the campaign and in the end, added jobs to our key campaign pledges.

When we discussed the question of a running mate later, he recommended that we pick someone who would bring credibility to the ticket on health or education, which were our key issues but that too, was not accepted. Ironically, we picked a banker who could not help but bring more attention to the economy.

When we started focusing on Health and education, the numbers started moving up and the campaign got traction.

Every few months, Larry would visit and we would go over the polls and other questions of strategy.

Another strong recommendation was that of putting more women and younger people around the candidate. He said he had examined many pictures of the candidate and found very few women or young people in them. Most of them were filled with old men. He said the candidate would look more attractive if surrounded more often by women and young people.

With that we started designing adverts highlighting education and healthcare.

Despite this commitment, it was difficult to get the candidate and other key speakers to focus on these messages. While his speeches tried to focus on these key issues, supporting speakers tended to veer off from these key messages.

One of the things we never could decide and implement was to get the balance in advertising right. Since there was no effective centralized control, people fought for what they were comfortable with or stood to gain from. The result was that people who worked in outdoor advertising were mostly pushing outdoor advertising while those who worked with T.V. and radio were always pushing those. An exception to this was Geddy Laryea who felt that we needed to have an overall budget and then assign percentages to the various types of advertising.

THE RAWLINGS FACTOR

One area where we all disagreed with Larry was that he believed former President Rawlings was a decided asset to the NDC and that we should not attack him. According to Larry, most Ghanaians saw Rawlings as someone who came with the gun and left us in peace, with democracy. To us, we felt that he was a decided liability and that the more he was involved in the campaign, the better it was for us.

Our information from the NDC was that they wanted President Rawlings to keep as low a profile as possible. We learned that when he took to traveling around, the NDC people were worried. On our side, we were ecstatic.

Our view seemed to be supported indirectly by Ben Ephson recently when he indicated in his view picking John Mahama against the wishes of President Rawlings had been very helpful to Professor Mills. Ben Ephson indicated that picking John Mahama despite the opposition of Mr Rawlings and his wife had helped Prof. Mills prove that he was his own man.

CAMPAIGN STRATEGY

Sometime after our conversation with Larry, the campaign team met for Dr. Kofi Konadu Apraku to present his proposed strategy to the campaign team.

The VISION, in summary was to hold to what we had and seek to make new gains. This meant holding the 128 seats we had, retaining the Presidency and picking up new seats.

As he himself indicated in the introduction, this had been prepared mainly by him with some inputs from the investigative reports of the NPP research committee under Brigadier Odei and the opinions of some regional executives.

In the document, he projected that we would increase our support in virtually every region. For example, he projected that in the Presidential elections, we would increase our percentage of the votes from 75% to 78% in Ashanti, while in the Central Region, we were expected to increase our support from 58 to 59%. In the Parliamentary elections, it was projected that we could retain about 115 to 125 seats for sure and be very competitive in another 25. To sum up, we were expecting to win the Presidential poll "ONE TOUCH" while picking up Parliamentary seats in virtually every region.

When he finished he was challenged on his projections for some regions and for some of the seats.

For example, I felt that projections for our performance in the Central Region, both for Presidential and Parliamentary were too optimistic. I explained that Professor Mills had spent a lot of time in the preceding two years building bridges to the region and that Dr. Nduom was expected to put up quite a respectable showing in the region. Furthermore, there was a sense of disappointment in the region that despite giving us victories in 2000 and 2004, they had gotten nothing in return. I felt that given those three reasons, it was unrealistic to expect that we would improve on our 2004 performance in the Central Region. On Ashanti, I felt that it was unrealistic to expect that Nana Akufo-Addo could outperform President Kufuor in the President's home region. Ironically, we all accepted that Nana Akufo-Addo would outperform President Kufuor in the Eastern region and we turned out to be wrong. Dan Botwe and Mac Manu disagreed with Dr Apraku on the projections for Parliamentary seats in quite a few regions and were very persuasive. In the constituency by constituency analysis, the methods used were not rigorous and consistent. As a result, sometimes, there was strong support for some candidates who were not popular and decided opposition from party leaders to candidates who turned out to be very strong. For instance, there were strong signals from the ground that NPP activists did not like our candidates for Nkawkaw, Bosome-Freho, Bekwai and Upper Denkyira but the party leadership was unmoved. In Navrongo Central, the party leadership felt that Kofi Adda was weak but Rita Asobayire was unbending in his defense. "If we win one seat in Upper East, it will be Navrongo Central. The Chiefs and some big people, including the Vice-President do not like him but the masses in Navrongo love Kofi and will carry him to victory," she predicted. Kofi Adda won. Mac Manu and Dan Botwe, during these discussions were very knowledgeable about local conditions in the various constituencies.

THE CANDIDATE'S SCHEDULE

One thing we over-emphasized was the candidate's own campaign. Directing resources to support the candidate's tours was always considered a priority. This was re-enforced by the realisation that wherever the candidate went, there was increase in our support and the enthusiasm of our supporters.

This perception led us to keep the candidate on the road month after month. One effect of this was that the excitement generated made everyone more determined to be in the candidate's entourage. Nana Akufo-Addo kept a punishing schedule. It was not unusual to have him finish a day at one a.m. and start the next day at six a.m. with meetings. From sun-up to sun-down, there was an endless stream of people who needed to see the candidate and he saw them all. This was in direct contradiction of the public perception that he was inaccessible.

In retrospect, it appears that the candidate spent too much time in certain regions, particularly the Volta Region and the Northern regions. More of the candidate's time should have been spent changing minds in Greater Accra, Central Region and in his own Eastern region as well as driving up enthusiasm in the Ashanti Region.

Generally, about a week before the candidate would visit a region, staff of the Danquah Institute would visit the region to interact with party elders and identify key issues. These issues would go into a briefing book for the candidate. In addition to this, the staff of Danquah Institute helped with research for speeches.

I remember once being assigned to give a speech on Sanitation and the Environment. After driving by in the morning to tell Atobra, Brenda and Adelaide the information that I needed, they researched the information while I drove to Kumasi. I got there with a little over an hour to go for the speech. With their information and some superb support work from my Special Assistant, Kofi Karikari, we got together a speech that was very well received. The Danquah staff, led ably by Gabby, Perry Okudzeto and Sophia Korkor, also did a very good job in monitoring the airways and doing whatever was needed, despite poor co-ordination that got in the way of effectiveness.

During the visits, the main activity was rallies. Time and time again, Larry suggested that we should move away from that format and do more interactions, with market women, workers, teachers and students. In Sefwi-Wiawso for instance, we managed to hold a forum where ordinary people asked questions. While it was a success, it was almost scuttled at the last minute. Unknown to Gabby Otchere Darko and I who were planning it, throughout the night, people got to the candidate to warn him about how bad this idea was since it was likely that the public would embarrass him with unexpected questions. As the event got underway, the candidate was very nervous and did not look very comfortable. The event came off without a hitch and was judged as very successful by the public as well as the media that was present. The next week, a similar event planned for Hohoe was scuttled after objections by local party leaders.

INTERVIEWS

During the first round, there were very few interviews by the candidate.

However, he had some very good ones with "PEACE FM" and some print media, notably the "DAILY GRAPHIC". Perhaps his best interview was his appearance on "MAA NKOMO", before an audience of women. While he came across very well during interviews, it was always a difficult task getting Nana to do interviews.

On one occasion, after recommendations that we start opening up the campaign to the media, we arranged an interview with Metro T.V. on "GOOD EVENING GHANA". However with a few hours to go for the interview, Nana Akufo-Addo decided he did not feel like having the interview. Jake Obetsebi Lamptey got on the phone to try and persuade him to change his mind but he was unsuccessful. Gabby Otchere Darko and I had followed Nana Akufo-Addo to the wake for the late former Speaker of Parliament, Honourable Peter Ala Adjetey, where he explained that after being at the wake, he just did not feel like having an interview that evening.

During the second round, we had interviews at virtually every step.

SEPERATION FROM THE GOVERNMENT

During the campaign, I and a few others repeatedly raised with the Presidential candidate the question of if and under what circumstances the campaign would disagree with the government. I was the leading advocate of what is generally called "pragmatic separation". We were advocating that there were circumstances under which a campaign should separate from its own government. I had watched George W. Bush in 2000, win the votes of moderates by disagreeing with the largely conservative Republican Congress. As he put it "I believe that the Republican Congress should not balance our budget on the backs of the poor." In my judgment, I believed that the campaign should have distanced itself from things like the "Jubilee House" and the Presidential jets. I believe Boakye Agyarko agreed with that idea. The candidate was steadfastly opposed to the suggestion. As he put it "I have been a member of this administration from day one and I am not going to separate myself from it . It is a matter of principle to me and I cannot bend on that." Recently, when I raised that with Nana , he said that while this theory might work in other places, "here, it would not be understood They will say that you are admitting the President you are trying to succeed is not a good President and that will doom your campaign."

MOVING IN THE POLLS

Despite the difficulties, by September, our internal polls showed that we were ahead and heading for a first round victory. This lead was also evidenced by other polls. The various polls had us getting 49% to 53% of the votes, with the NDC on an average of 8 to 10 points behind. Interestingly, quite a number of NDC functionaries appeared to believe that we were winning. In private moments, they confessed that they hoped to pick up some seats and to push the Presidential ballot to a second round. Indeed, after the first round, I met NDC members who were ecstatic that the Presidential poll was going to the second round. This meant that despite the effort, time and resources spent by the NDC in vilifying our candidate, he was ahead in the polls. While many talked about Nana Addo's so-called elitist image and how he was "born with a silver-spoon in his mouth.", no candidate for President since Nkrumah had had more legitimate populist credentials. He had been one of the major leaders of the People's Movement for Freedom and Justice that opposed the Acheampong dictatorship, he had worked to free AFRC convicts through the courts and he had marched at the head of the "Kumi Preko" demonstrations that challenged the PNDC/NDC regimes in their dying days.

HOUSE TO HOUSE CAMPAIGNING

The importance of house-to-house campaigning was not lost on any of us. Indeed, the efficacy of house to house or village to village campaigning had been demonstrated beyond doubt by President Kufuor who, between 1998 and 2000, visited virtually every hamlet , village and town in Ghana. There were heartwarming stories of villages pledging to vote for the " Gentle giant" because "since independence, you are the first person running for President to visit this village". In 2008, we had difficulty doing that for a number of reasons. First, given the time our candidate was chosen, there was just not enough time for the Presidential candidate to do that. President Mills, after all, was building on the work he had done from the 2000 and the 2004 elections. Second, too many people who could have been very effective campaigning in their districts or constituencies preferred being in the candidate's convoy to being in their regions or constituencies.

FLOATERS VERSUS " THE BASE"

Throughout the campaign, one difficulty we had was in defining our primary audience. While some, like me believed that we needed to focus mostly on floating voters and floating regions, others believed in playing to our base. Some believed that we should hit the NDC hard on its lapses while in office and tie them to the PNDC while defending our record aggressively. To them, it was "my party, right or wrong and no concessions on anything". This division led to some confusion as to which faces to put forward from the campaign. If you believed in "my party right or wrong" you preferred certain radio and T.V. personalities. If you believed in reaching for the centre, you preferred others. Indeed, where one stood on this issue affected one's preference for events. The people who preferred to play to our base preferred rallies and predominantly party events. In the higher echelons of the campaign, I was repeatedly taken to task for being "too soft".

As I pointed out, there was nothing courageous about pounding the table in the safe confines of a studio sitting across from Hannah Tetteh, Alex Segbefia or even Ama Benyiwa Doe. Pounding the table in a studio, frankly, in my view was just bad manners masquerading as courage. From this strategy, I would have preferred putting out on a more consistent basis, people like Madam Oboshie Sai, Jake Obetsebi Lamptey, Prof Frimpong Boateng, Kwamena Duncan, Nana Akomeah, Papa Owusu Ankomah and Andy Awuni.

The value of having more low-key congenial faces for the campaign was dramatically brought home to me after the campaign when I visited a village near Wenchi. We were surrounded by a group of young men, from both NPP and NDC. When I inquired how the elections had gone in the village, they said the NPP had lost both the first and the second rounds. However, we had cut the deficit of a hundred votes in the first round by a little more than half during the second round. When I asked how that had happened, one young man explained that it was due to Auntie Rosemary who came from Wenchi to campaign in the second round. As he said in halting twi "Ono de ondidi atem.

Wakasa kyere obiara. NPP mpaninfo dee aka no, wadidi yen atem"
. The translation was that Madam Rosemary had been friendly and
respectful in dealing with everybody while other NPP leaders tended
to insult them.   We cannot, for years to come, win elections by just
focusing on our base. There are just not enough of us. We need to
bring enough floaters and independents to give us victories in the years
ahead, just as we did in 2000 and again in 2004.

NDC STRATEGY

On the NDC side, a "NATIONAL CAMPAIGN READINESS
PLAN" was put together as far back as 2006. Amongst other things,
the plan called for reaching out to the security forces, dealing with
its image as a party lacking in internal democracy and reaching out
to the smaller parties for alliances. Also during the formulation of
this plan it was decided to emphasize propaganda and to exploit the
perceived weaknesses of the NPP. Another of the critical things the
NDC decided to do was to also undermine the confidence and the
credibility of the Electoral Commission. Indeed, the European Union
Election Observation Mission to Ghana stated in its report that "As part
of its tendency to accuse all state institutions of overt bias, the NDC
constantly criticized the Electoral Commission for lack of impartiality
without any substantial grounds for many of its allegations."

Throughout the elections there was a very deliberate strategy to
restrict Prof. Mills mainly to Greater Accra, Central and Western
Regions. Indeed, there are nearly thirty constituencies in Ashanti
Region that President Mills never visited after 2006.

Finally, the NDC seemed determined to heighten the atmosphere of
insecurity in the country during the period leading up to the elections.
On this, the EU team reported that "During the period immediately
preceding the election on the 28th December, 2008, as part of growing
tension, both the Chairman of the Electoral Commission and the
Director of Election Operations received threats by telephone from
anonymous callers,". While those behind these calls were not identified,

given the level of invective directed at the EC by the NDC, it is likely that those behind these calls were probably elements associated with the NDC.

CHAPTER NINE
THE IEA EVENTS

"Elections are always about the future, not the past."

Former US President Bill Clinton

THE INSTITUTE OF ECONOMIC AFFAIRS, IEA, was established in 1989 as a policy think-tank and has become over the years, the most influential NGO on our governance as well as a major catalyst for interaction by actors across the political divide leading to collective action to solve problems.

The IEA's mission includes:

- The promotion of good governance in Ghana

- The establishment of multi-party democracy in Ghana and,

- The creation of a free and fair market economy in Ghana, the West Africa sub-region and the entire African continent.

To attain these objectives, the IEA:

- Provides a forum/platform for the exchange of ideas

- Promotes research and publication on important economic, socio-economic political and legal issues

- Provides training to institutions of democracy such as Parliament, the Judiciary, the media and Civil society

-Promotes the use of economic reasoning with particular regard to scarcity and trade-offs

-Monitors and provides in-depth analysis on the establishment of democracy

-Serves as a nerve-center of policy analysis and public education.

Right from the beginning of the year, the IEA started organizing events around the campaign to improve the conduct, the atmosphere and the flow of information to the public. These events were consistent with what the IEA had done to facilitate the return and growth of Democracy.

TRANSITIONS IN OUR DEMOCRACY

Early in the year, they organized a workshop on Presidential transitions at Atimpoku. It brought together representatives of the major political parties and some experts, together with the media to examine our transition process in the light of our experiences. The workshop was chaired by Col. Agyemfra and facilitated very well by the IEA staff, led by Mrs Jean Mensa. In addition to a prepared background paper, there were presentations by Mr. P.V. Obeng of the NDC and this writer, from the NPP side. Mr Obeng discussed the 2001 transition while I discussed external transitions and the lessons learned. In my address, I warned that looking at our transitional arrangements, we were sitting on a time-bomb. I said "First, in all probability, the transition period of Ghana and most other African is too short. In our particular case, if ever there is both a second round and a dispute in a Presidential election, it is likely that our system may be unable to withstand both and have an inauguration on schedule." Afterwards, there was a very lively discussion of our transition and what could be done about it. The time-bomb I predicted almost came to pass in 2009. We agreed that the first round of elections should be on November 7ᵗʰ with a run-off, if needed, on November 28ᵗʰ. There were also proposals on Parliament electing a Speaker before inauguration day and the preparation of hand-over notes.

VIOLENCE IN OUR POLITICS

They followed this up a few months later when they organized a retreat attended by all the parties with representation in Parliament to discuss ways of reducing violence in our campaigns. The group reviewed a similar document signed by the parties in 2004 and looked for ways to improve it. In the end, the representatives signed a very good document. On our way to the agreement, however, a lot of accusations were traded, particularly between the NDC and the NPP. In the end, the parties signed a document called "THE POLITICAL PARTIES CODE OF CONDUCT 2008". For example, under CAMPAIGNING, the final document stated "6: Political Parties, their members, agents and supporters should adhere to the "PUBLIC ORDER ACT 1994." In this regard, Party Officials shall co-ordinate their campaign activities in such a way that no two political parties shall hold public meetings or rallies in the same locality on the same day, if such meetings or rallies are likely to be so close to each other that a possibility of creating conflict arises."In view of the acrimony and violence that were later witnessed in the campaign, it seems the agreements reached by the parties were honoured mainly in the breach by the political parties.

MEDIA AND POLITICS

One of the most informative of these sessions involved the media and its role in our democracy. Held on the last week-end of March, it brought together many seasoned journalists for a very serious discussion on the role of the media in our campaigns.

Prof. Kwame Karikari of the School of Communications reminded the audience that while thinking about objectivity and fairness, it bears remembering that the origins of the media itself had been adversarial and partisan.

Mr. Boadu Ayeboafoh of "THE DAILY GRAPHIC" was also in good form as he quoted Joseph Pulitzer that "A journalist is the lookout on the ship of state. He notes the passing sail, the little things of interest that dot the horizon in fine weather. He reports the drifting castaways whom the ship can save. He peers through the fog and storm to give warnings of damages ahead. He is not thinking of his wages or the profits of his owners. He is there to watch over the safety and welfare of those who trust him." In view of the rabid partisanship and irresponsibility that was exhibited by some in the Press, that weekend pointed to challenges that the media were unable to address during the election year.

EVENING ENCOUNTER WITH CANDIDATES

In June, the IEA, in collaboration with the GBC and other organizations, organized what was dubbed as "AN EVENING ENCOUNTER WITH THE CANDIDATES".

Every candidate of a party with representation in Parliament made some remarks followed by questions from the audience.

Whenever there was such an event, we focused mainly on the NDC.

Prof Mills went first and spent most of his address attacking the NPP record. We felt that was a mistake and spent some time making sure Nana Akufo-Addo's remarks focused more on the future.

To prepare the address, we had a series of meetings. The day before the encounter, we met to agree on the final outline of the address. It was felt that the remarks should be delivered extempore with notes only. The next morning, we reconvened. After reading through the draft I had prepared, Nana Akufo-Addo stated that he wished to read the prepared text rather than speak extempore. With that, everyone wanted to make an input. To add insult to injury, many did not bother to read the draft. We spent a lot of time discussing things that had already been settled either in our draft manifesto or in earlier meetings.

With time running out, some would lapse into anecdotes which, while entertaining, were not relevant to the task at hand. In the end, we ran out of time. Nana Akufo-Addo left for the event while Gabby Otchere Darko, Krantemaa and I struggled to finish the speech. In the address, he began by touting the NPP's achievements in government, saying "First, the NPP government has given this nation its best economy in our half-century of independence. We have achieved macro-economic stability for longest period in our history. We have reduced significantly both interest rates and inflation while nearly quadrupling the size of our economy to US 15 billion in the first seven years of the NPP". Then he took on those who claimed things have worsened under the NPP."You are better off if you are one of the millions of Ghanaians who have been freed from the clutches the "cash-and-carry" system by the National Health Insurance Scheme. Your family is better off if your young child is benefitting from the School Feeding Program and/or the Capitation Grant and your older child now has a chance to attend University or Polytechnic because of the expansion in facilities that has led to increased enrollment.

You are better off when the road in your area has been improved and travel takes less time than before."

He laid out a comprehensive vision for moving the country forward. He then concluded by stating "We need to take a firm step into the future if we are to be part of the rapidly changing global village with its technological advancements.

I shall lead by example through a hands-on approach, working around the clock to restore the culture of hard work.

I shall create an effective and efficient public service that delivers to the expectation of our people.

I will be action-oriented, demanding of results, chase progress and not tolerate bureaucratic inertia.

I have a strong desire to serve Ghana with clear conscience, pure motives and solid character. I will offer a leadership of competence, courage, compassion and commitment.

From Pusiga to Axim, from Hamile to Keta, we all by fate are Ghanaians first. We have to emphasize the things that bring us together. I believe in Ghana and I ask you also to believe in Ghana. We are moving forward. Yenko yanim. Yenko yanim! Wonya wor hie!

And with God as our guide, we shall succeed.

God bless you. God bless Ghana."

The speech was received very well but the questions and answers revealed that while the candidate was very well-informed, his answers were a tad too long.

Most observers agreed that Nana Akufo-Addo had clearly won this round but we needed to get his answers more succinct.

In a report in the "DAILY GRAPHIC" on June 25th, the paper reported that many people had found the exercise useful but wanted the candidates to address certain issues, particularly, jobs.

THE IEA DEBATES

The next series of events were the debates. Since many touted Nana Addo's courtroom skills and his eloquence, I assumed that our team would be looking forward to the debates. It was therefore a surprise when I discovered that many in the campaign, including some key people, were not keen on the debates.

They argued that in a debate between the NPP and all the opposition parties, the opposition would gang up against our candidate and attack him. "We will just be a sitting target for the opposition during the debate"

Those of us on the other side argued that it would be unacceptable for the NPP Candidate to duck out of the debates. The nation, we argued, expected a debate and these have become a rite of passage in our democracy. Someone on the other side asserted "Mills did not debate in 2000 and Kufuor did not do so in 2004." In response, I pointed out that in 2000, Mills had lost and that in 2004, Kufuor was President already. To address the issue of others ganging up on our candidate, we planned that we would agree to a debate of candidates of parties with representation in parliament. This would limit the debate to the NPP's Nana Akufo-Addo, the NDC's Prof. Mills, the CPP's Dr. Nduom and the PNC's Dr. Mahama.

With Cardinal Turkson in the Chair, and the NDC and CPP represented by Alex Segbefia and David Ampofo respectively, our proposals were quickly accepted.

To address the concerns about ganging up on our candidate, I suggested a "Right of rebuttal" that would permit a candidate, if he felt his position had been misstated, to request a chance to state his position or correct the misrepresentation. This rebuttal would last no more than one minute. This too was accepted. One of the high-points of the preparation was the balloting for seating in the debates.

A few weeks earlier, Jake Obetsebi Lamptey had picked number one on the ballot, for the December poll. The night before the balloting, Nana Akufo- Addo had learned that Jake Obetsebi Lamptey picked the last spot for President Kufuor in 2000. He therefore asked him to pick for him. When he picked number one, many read that as a good omen.

When I followed that by picking number one for the debate seating, morale went even higher.

After I reported to the campaign on the negotiations, I was sent to also request that a table   be used for the debate.

Throughout all this, the IEA staff, the debate committee and all the parties worked together very well. It was always a pleasure to deal with Cardinal Turkson, Mrs. Jean Mensa and her staff as well as the other parties. The Cardinal has an excellent sense of humour and is very affable.

The first debate occurred on Wednesday, 29th October, in Accra. There was a comic moment when Dr Nduom, answering a question on pensions, cited Zimbabwe as a place where a pension is paid to a person the day she or he dies. Dr. Nduom was generally believed to have put in the best performance.

As the CHRONICLE reported "TRACENDENTAL NDUOM CONNECTS", many in the public believed the CPP candidate had won the debate.

While Nana Akufo-Addo's answers were good, he had been advised to look at the moderators while answering questions and this made him seem as if he was not addressing the television audience. Furthermore, based on the advice of our experts, he had worn a suite that was too dark.

In contrast, Nduom was dressed in Kente and jumper and his answers, while not deep, were crisp and very populist.

Afterwards, there was a bit of recrimination in our camp. I was blamed for not being tough enough in the debate negotiation while others came in for criticism for giving the candidate bad technical advice.

Ironically, because his answers were so detailed, some complained that Nana Akufo-Addo had advance knowledge of the questions. While that was quickly debunked, that charge was in a sense, a back-handed compliment to the thoroughness with which our team had prepared him. To begin the preparation, I went over all the questions the identifiable groups had asked the candidates during the "EVENING ENCOUNTER WITH THE IEA". Working from these areas of interest, I prepared 15 questions and answers for the first meeting.

After the first mock questions, these answers were further refined with the candidate's input and he spent time reading over the answers we had all agreed to.

SPY IN OUR MIDST

One strange episode was when we learned after the first debate that the mock questions that had been used to prepare our candidate was in NDC hands within hours of our meeting. The obvious implication was that there was a spy in our midst. It was this set of mock questions that formed the basis of the NDC claim that Nana had an advance knowledge of the questions for the debate. Unfortunately, this was not the first time information that was confidential had ended up in NDC hands. In the early parts of the campaign, we had discussed in some detail, the candidates personal habits, including his dressing. That discussion and the notes made by some of our key participants, was in NDC hands within a few days. Eventually, one staffer was identified as the likely source of these leaks but was allowed to work throughout the campaign because some in the campaign vouched for her integrity. The effect of this was that it reinforced the penchant for secrecy amongst some in the campaign. With the excuse that there were spies in our midst, people were denied access to information that could have made them more effective.

For the second debate, we were joined in the preparation by Edward Boateng who brought a lot of professionalism to the task. Sometimes though, things went a little overboard. In Tamale, we even got an exact replica of the chairs used in the actual debate for the candidate to practice sitting in our "mock session"

The second debate was on November 12th in Tamale. Security was very tight.

The second debate covered the economy and issues of peace and security and many believed that Nana Akufo-Addo was the clear winner.

The highlight of the debate in was towards the end when the moderator asked the candidates to make a pledge for peace.

Presidential Candidates just before Tamale debate. From R to L; Prof. Mills, Mr. Akufo-Addo & Dr. Nduom.

IEA Administrator Mrs. Jean Mensa greets NPP Presidential Candidate Nana Akufo-Addo just before Tamale debate.

For both debates, Mrs. Mensa and the I.E.A. staff were very helpful. Each time someone in our campaign had a question and I did not have the answer readily, they were very helpful.

Cardinal Turkson, Chair of IEA Debate team makes point to author before debate.

One of the interesting side-effects was the distribution of tickets. It led to much finger-pointing and frustration when people who thought they were entitled to tickets did not get them while others who were less well-known got them. To some, it seemed that their prestige would suffer irreparable damage if they did not get tickets to the debate.

Nana Akufo-Addo makes point during IEA Debate

Presidential Candidates hold hands in pledge for peace during Tamale debate on Nov. 12th, 2008

THE VICE-PRESIDENTIAL DEBATE

After the Presidential debates, we were approached for a Vice-Presidential debate.

While I and many in the campaign felt that a Vice-Presidential debate was an anti-climax after the two Presidential debates, some, particularly in Dr. Bawumia's team wanted it. In the end, Nana supported them and I was directed to negotiate for a Vice-Presidential debate if possible.

For the meeting, I was joined by Jake Obetsebi Lamptey. After some negotiation, we agreed to accept the same guidelines and moderators for the Presidential debates.

The team that prepared Dr. Bawumia for the debate was led by Jake and included Yoofi Grant, Gabby Otchere Darko and myself. Dr. Bawumia was a good study and very pleasant to work with.

The Vice-Presidential debate was seen as a success by many and all the candidates acquitted themselves well.

EVALUATING THE IEA EVENTS

In my opinion, the I.E.A. events are a very important part of our electioneering process.

While the public is understandably focused mostly on the debates, the other events are equally important. For instance, the meetings that discussed election violence, the press and our transitional arrangements were just as important to our democracy as the debates.

First they help bring the parties together and thus help in fostering understanding amongst the parties. Personally, it was very useful for me to get to meet leaders of other parties, like Dr. Kwabena Adjei, Alhaji Ramadan, Ivor Greenstreet, P.V. Obeng and E.T. Mensah.

Secondly, by organizing the Evening Encounter and the debates, they help to put the candidates on the same platform and thus to assist the public in comparing them.

On the debates themselves, while very useful, they were too long. They should be limited to about 90 minutes. One of the factors that made them long was the follow-up questions by the moderators. While they were only meant to help prompt the candidate where his/her initial response was not clear, it became routine and thus wasted time.

Another factor that lengthened the debates was the fact that the candidates exceeded the time limits too often and the judges were too lax in enforcing the time limits.

While from anecdotal evidence, the debates were valuable, it would be helpful to undertake a scientific poll to determine the number of viewers and how many were influenced by them.

In retrospect, it would also be very helpful if the forum and publicity for the presentation of the manifestos were organized in a standard form by the IEA.

Also, the IEA and other similar organizations should consider teaming up to do exit polling. It will help us know how the different age-groups and genders vote.

Finally, I think it is inappropriate to have a Vice-Presidential debate after the Presidential debates.

The Vice-Presidential debate must be scheduled between the Presidential debates.

CHAPTER TEN
CAMPAIGNING

"All politics is local"

Former US House of Representatives Speaker, Thomas Tip O'Neil

AFTER THE NOMINATION WAS WON, THE first task of the campaign was to heal the breaches in the party and to re-assure the foot-soldiers who were complaining about neglect by party leaders.

In addition to a thank you tour, the campaign committee made two very crucial decisions.

THE PARTY-GOVERNMENT RELATIONS COMMITTEE

The first was the establishment of the "PARTY-GOVERNMENT RELATIONS COMMITTEE". As the candidate indicated during the inauguration, many in the party were not happy with how the government had related to the party and party members. Historically, many in the party yearned for the accessibility that party members reportedly had to Dr. Busia and his Ministers. According to legend, Dr. Busia spent every Thursday afternoon at the party headquarters where ordinary party members could schedule appointments to see him.

Unfortunately, with our return to power in 2001, that practice had not been revived. That committee was under the Chairmanship of Mr. Akenteng Appiah-Menka, a party elder. Indeed, during the primary, the reported neglect of party members by our government came up repeatedly. I had the opportunity to discuss party morale and leadership with former Chairman Mr. Da Rocha and Party Administrator Mr. Antwi-Adjei. Mr. Da Rocha spoke longingly of Dr. Busia's accessibility and how easy it had been to do business with him. He said that as General Secretary, while he was Busia's junior by far in age, he never felt intimidated engaging the Prime Minister in debate. On his part, Mr. Antwi-Adjei recalled fondly the days when President Kufuor, then the party nominee for the Presidency, used to frequent party headquarters. In those days, about 1999, the candidate would stop by his office on his way to the General Secretary's office and ask him how the staff was doing. The result was that Mr. Kufuor was exceptionally well-informed about the state of the party and its organs. He also recalled that during the nineties, during elections, Party Headquarters was the place to be. In the event, the Appiah-Menka committee did some work but due to the election results, implementation will have to await the return of NPP into government.

VISITS TO ORPHAN CONSTITUENCIES

The campaign itself started with visits to orphan constituencies after lightening "thank-you" tours to all regions. These visits, while gingering up interests in the orphan constituencies frustrated those in our strongholds to no end. They felt that the campaign was wasting time in areas where we had very little chance of doing well while neglecting strongholds.

Mostly, the campaigning consisted of the candidate having a continuous schedule of rallies. These rallies were invariable preceded with visits to the traditional rulers. These visits took an inordinate amount of time with endless speeches. Most of the traditional rulers praised the candidate and his party directly or indirectly. There was one episode in Tema where the NPP Candidate visited a traditional ruler and was praised fulsomely. The following week, the NDC Candidate visited the same traditional ruler and was praised just as enthusiastically.

One traditional ruler whose remarks really made an impression was the Asantehene, Otumfuo Osei Tutu II. He urged politicians to serve the people. He drew attention to the issue of development and urged politicians to promote peace. He urged the NPP Candidate to involve the young people in the party who had new ideas for moving the country forward.

When we filed forward to greet him individually, he had words of encouragement. He urged me to continue putting out ideas and assured me that the nation was hearing me. It was a pleasant surprise to hear that from him.

VISITS TO SCHOOLS

One part of campaigning that was very interesting was visiting schools. There was enthusiasm. Mostly, there were formal speeches but questions and answers were rare. There were such speeches at KNUST, UCC, UDS and Accra Poly.

Towards the end, the candidate delivered an Education speech at Accra Poly that was very well attended. The hall was over-crowded and hot. As Nana Akufo-Addo got ready to speak, the students started cheering. With the bad acoustics, it was difficult to hear him. As they kept cheering in excitement, he wondered whether they were trying to prevent him from speaking and wondered whether the event should be cancelled.

In time, he was reassured that the noise was really cheers of love and the events continued.

Of the campus speeches the two that got the best receptions were those at KNUST on energy and the one at UDS in Tamale on the Northern Development Authority and Fund.

One effect of spending so much time in areas we had lost is that we had less time to spend in the areas we had won. In the end for instance, we were forced to make virtue out of necessity by claiming that even though Nana Akufo-Addo had only visited the Central Region twice compared to eight by Prof. Mills, we still hoped to win Central Region.

INTERACTIVE EVENTS

Towards the end, we started blending interactive events with market-women, teachers and students into our visits. Unfortunately, local party leaders by and large, preferred rallies to these events that put the candidate directly in touch with ordinary people. Nich Adi Daku, the Director of Operations for the Campaign, really tried to schedule the candidate for these events but it was an uphill task.

In many places, the candidate, with the exception of the first events, was invariably late. At many stops, more people wanted to speak than was necessary and most spoke for too long.

Aside from the few local people selected to speak, the main speakers were the candidate, Alan Kyerematen, Kwabena Agyapong and Osafo Maafo. Once, when I joined the team in Brong-Ahafo, we realized after some time that towns on the candidate's itinerary had been kept waiting for a long time because the team had fallen behind schedule. Boakye-Agyarko and the Brong Ahafo Regional Minister, Ignatius Baafour Awuah joined me and a few others in going ahead of the convoy to speak to those waiting for the candidate. Some of the "prima-donnas" refused to do advanced work. They insisted on staying with the candidate and having their two minutes on the stage while the candidate was there. It was very encouraging to see first-hand, the willingness of the Regional Minister , Dr Kofi Barimah and Boakye-Agyarko to do whatever it took to get things done. Because of the many stops, most of the days were long. It was common to have the last rallies at night.

Effectiveness of events varied from place to place. In the Northern Region, Clifford Braimah, the Regional Organizer, once he returned to join the campaign was considered the go-to guy while nation-wide, Alhaji Short was considered perhaps the best Regional Chairman.

The Central Regional team was energetically and resourcefully led by Hon. Kennedy Agyapong with Alhaji Gibrine bringing years of experience to bear and Kwamena Duncan providing on-air presence. However, the team was hampered by divisions that started in the primary season and were never effectively dealt with. In Ajumako-Enyan-Essiam, for instance, the defeated incumbent and former Regional Minister, Hon. Isaac Edumadze was never reconciled to the campaign after losing the primary to Arthur Baiden. There were repeated reports, heatedly denied by Edumadze that he was supporting the independent candidate. Also in my own constituency, Abura-Asebu-Kwamankese, the defeated incumbent, Honourable Andrew Mensah was never effectively brought into the campaign. Since he had some following in the constituency, it made things very difficult for the new candidate, Maxwell Baidoo to get traction on the ground. We lost both seats.

In the Brong-Ahafo Region, three people who were very effective on the platform were Hon. MP "Abodwese" , Koranteng, Chairman for Pru constituency, also known as "Ebewura" or "proverb owner" and the Regional Organizer, Kwabena Darko. Of the "proverb-owner" one could truly say that he spoke in proverbs.

In Ashanti, whenever Kan Dapaah was available, he was effective. He also brought on board one of the most effective and celebrated grassroots organizers of the party in the region, Victor Owusu Jnr. Victor, together with the Deputy Regional Minister, Osei Asibey were the fulcrums around which the campaign in the region turned. Together with a few others, they worked to hold things together with Lawyer Owusu Afriyie, AKA "Sir John" leading their media assault. While it is commonly asserted that many of the Ashanti Region did not work very hard after their primary victories, there were exceptions. One of those praised for working very hard despite being assured of victory was Dr.

Matthew Prempeh, also known as "NAPO". Once, it was reported that upon hearing that "NAPO" was in the neighbourhood to campaign, an elderly lady who was in the shower just covered her body with cloth, soap and all and dashed out to see the "MANHYIA" candidate. Dr. Anane too, was reported to have worked very hard during the second round.

The fact that not much house-to-house was done in this campaign has become a cliché but even in this area, there were standouts. One such standout was Hon. Frema Opare of Ayawaso West Wugon who was so effective in room-to-room campaigning that her Legon constituents nicknamed her affectionately "THIRTY-NINE" because she was working like a thirty-nine year old.

On a few occasions, the last rallies occurred after midnight. These led to recriminations amongst local party officials and pleadings for the events to be rescheduled. Inevitably, some events had to be cancelled. By 6.00 a.m. the next morning, the team would be up and ready for another long day. Long before daylight, some women volunteers would be up to cook break-fast. Most of the time, this was rice, kenkey and some beverages.

These volunteers were particularly well-organised in Kumasi, Cape Coast, Sunyani and Tamale.

By the time we returned, they would have been at work for hours cooking supper. Supper was usually fufu, rice, kenkey and ampesi.

Sometimes, local party officials hosted the entourage by offering meals. In this, Alhaji Mustapha Idris, Alhaji Short and Patricia Appiagyei, together with some DCE's were stand-outs.

On the road, there was rarely time for lunch.

Throughout the campaign, the size of the candidate's entourage was always an issue. There were repeated complaints that at events, the local people were repeatedly crowded out. The large entourage led to long convoys and sometimes, accidents.

It also fostered the false belief that our campaign was a lavishly financed campaign. In fact, most of the vehicles did not belong to the campaign and were not fuelled by it. As the candidate said in response to one of the requests that he reduce his convoy, "how can I ask someone who has his own vehicle, is buying his own fuel and paying his own way and just wants to show support for me not to come along?"

Of course, the practical effect was that apart from the candidate's own team, we never had other teams to spread our message to other areas. The whole road campaign became the candidate's campaign. Unfortunately, while many could be reached by radio and T.V., many still want the candidate or other well-known party people to show up in their town or constituency. And our inexcusable failure to put quality teams in the field hurt our chances considerably. On the NDC side, for at least the last four months, they had teams in the field led by Professor Mills, John Mahama and former President Rawlings respectively and this made them very effective.

Nana greets nurses during the campaign

Nana interacts with market women on the campaign trail. Behind him is Prof. Mike Ocquaye.

THE MEDIA

Other areas of campaigning that were crucial were the newspapers, radio and T.V.

Most of the press were neutral and what we got out of them was going to depend on how much we put in.

While some of our people who went on the air were very effective, some were not.

Often, people were invited by the stations without the knowledge of the campaign and put us into some trouble. In other instances, we put people out there who were not well-informed enough.

One difficulty we had was that most of our big names, after years in government, were not as eager to go on air as they used to be. Thus, on the whole, the NDC had more big names on air than we did. The result was that those of us on air were stretched rather thin.

Even though a CPP member, Malik Kweku Baako was the foremost defender of the NPP government. He was very effective. Unfortunately, while he had access to documents and information, others who were not members of the government had a very difficult time getting access to documents.

Also, while most of the time, we did quite well in head-to-head confrontations, there were serious omissions and defects on our side.

First, too often, on PEACE FM and ADOM, which were the leading Akan stations in the nation, we sometimes sent or had invited people who could not speak any of the languages well. While such people would be excellent on Joy or Citi FM, sending them to Peace, Adom and Asempa FM stations was very ineffective.

Second, we never succeeded in engaging stations like Radio Gold and Obonu FM. I argued repeatedly that we should engage these stations. While no one objected in principle, we never actualized a plan to engage these stations. While I and a few others appeared on Radio Gold, I argued with some support, to even have them interview our candidate. However those scheduling the candidate never got around to making him available.

Throughout the campaign, we never agreed on who was the primary target of our advertising and media campaign. Some favoured the harsh, confrontational, "take-no-prisoners" approach while others favoured the moderate, respectful "throw-no-bombs" approach that appeals to floating voters, women and apolitical people. While the difference was not significant for instance in billboards, it mattered in terms of those who were put on air and how they came across to the public. Often after an appearance, while independents were calling to commend me for being reasonable and effective, party big-wigs would complain that "you did not go after them hard enough". From monitoring comments on the NDC presentations on air, it seemed that their most effective people were their moderates, Alex Segbefia and Hannah Tetteh. It seemed reasonable to me that from this our moderates would be most effective.

We got a lot of flak for bill-boards that were too big and too many. Part of why this happened was that the co-ordination of billboards was sometimes, not in the hand of professionals. This led to separate spates of billboards, sometimes funded by volunteers who wanted to see more of particular billboards or adverts.

Quite early in the campaign, there was a feeling that certain stations did not like us. Radio Gold was so deep into the NDC that it needs no discussion. However, it is surprising that in 2000, Radio Gold had been fairly objective in its coverage but turned decisively against us.

In the end, Radio Gold was virulently against us. Even the European Union Monitoring team, generally loath to criticize had this to say after stating that the media were generally fair," The one exception was "RADIO GOLD" that constantly criticized the NPP in its programming."

Before the second round, Radio Gold even played a concocted tape of voices that they claimed to be voices of NPP leaders plotting to take bodies to the Volta Region to help frame the NDC for the killing of NPP agents! However, given the strength of their audience and the fact that we could help increase their audience, we should have worked harder at getting our story onto Radio Gold. The few times I went on, their audience was very good. They asked very good questions.

It appeared to me that their audience at large was more balanced than the station.

JOY FM

One station that was interesting was Joy FM. Many in our campaign believed the station was against us and their staff vehemently denied these accusations.

In the middle of the campaign, they once invited the parties separately to discuss coverage and our concerns.

I explained that it seemed that while they were objective in their reporting, sometimes, in their choice of what to put on air and topics to be discussed in discussion problems, they appeared biased.

Two examples will suffice. When in the middle of a campaign, JOY FM chooses to discuss the death of Ghanaians in Gambia without recalling the history of a similar episode in the Ivory Coast under the NDC in which more people died, it would appear to casual observers that the station is out to put the NPP and its Candidate in bad light. Furthermore, if on a Saturday morning, three of the four topics picked for discussion on "NEWSFILE" put the NPP in bad light, it leads to the conclusion that the station is not well disposed towards our party.

Of course, Kofi Owusu and the Joy FM journalists defended their conduct passionately. In the end, they took our concerns on board and we noted their journalistic perspectives.

Despite these concerns, I have no doubt that Joy FM is probably the best station in the country in terms of quality. I certainly enjoyed interacting with their very fine staff and wish them well. Even when we did not like their reporting, I am sure they were doing their best to present as objective a view as possible.

Over the few days after the first round when the results were not clear, I spent a lot of time in their studios debating various NDC members, notably Hannah Tetteh and Alex Segbefia. I saw first-hand as Matilda Asante, Kojo Oppong Nkrumah, Araba Coomson, Sampson Lardy and others struggled to get the right results onto their board and out to the public and I was impressed by their professionalism.

PEACE FM

Peace fm, with the largest audience, was also very professional. They had one of the best programs for discussing the Manifestos of any station. Unfortunately, this program was in the afternoon when they do not have their largest audience. Whenever they called on their "Kokrokoo Show", to clarify something, their host, Kwame Sefa Kai, was very gracious, to the point and extremely professional.

The view that both "JOY FM" and "PEACE FM" was endorsed by the EU monitoring team reported that "Joy fm and Peace fm provided balanced coverage of the two political parties".

One station whose callers were surprising was Citi fm. After their meteoric rise to the top echelons and their very large audience, they were always in our minds. While their staff, including Bernard Avle, Richard Sky and Shamima Muslim were very professional and fair, the textors and callers generally gave us a hard time. There were repeated reports of the NDC organizing callers who congregated in one office and called the stations in rotation.

Oman fm was the new Big kid on the block. Fiifi and his crew there were very friendly and that station will only get bigger with time.

While we are overtly focused on Accra stations, there are very influential stations in the regions. For instance, stations in Kumasi, like Angel, Kesben and Ash are very influential. Indeed, Kwame Adinkra of Angel is probably as influential as any of the Accra hosts.

In the Central Region, the stations to listen to or focus on were Radio Central and Ahomka fm and an interview with Kojo Quansah was quite an event.

NEWSPAPERS

As for the newspapers, one could not afford to ignore even the smallest of them. A newspaper might sell only fifty copies but if it had a damaging story against your candidate on page one picked up by a major station like Joy FM or Peace FM for the newspaper review, it became more important than having a positive story on the back or inside pages of the "Daily Graphic" which was not reviewed. It also became apparent very quickly that if an accusation in print is denied on air once, that is not enough. Three days after it was denied on-air in Accra, it would be the stuff of newspaper reviews in Bolga, Tamale and Wa and could be just as damaging as when it first appeared in Accra. It therefore became very important to get the campaign's point of view to the various newspaper editors as quickly as possible. Unfortunately for us, too many of our key people did not like answering their phones. This sometimes led to situations where reporters as well as some even in our campaign had no access to the people with first-hand information about an issue at stake.

THE DCE's

As in every campaign, local issues and the candidates mattered. In many places, DCE's were seen by the public as the face of the party and where they were unpopular, the voters punished the party for their perceived arrogance. For example, in the Central Region, a few days before the second round, Jake Obetsebi Lamptey, Kwamena Bartels and I met the Regional House of Chiefs to persuade them to support the NPP. During the meeting, one Chief reminded us that the DCE's were our primary links with the people and that in many instances; our party had been ill-served by our DCE's. He said that on many occasions, he had tried to see the DCE for his area and been unsuccessful. However, while he was waiting to see the DCE, young women, scantily dressed were waltzing in and out of the DCE's office. This account was backed by many of the assembled chiefs.

With regards to local issues, some of the issues that hurt us very badly along the coastal belt were our mismanagement or failure to manage pre-mix fuel and our seeming indifference to the issue of pair-trawling. For some unknown reasons, Honourable Nana Atto Arthur and Honourable Gladys Asmah, who needed to collaborate to resolve the issue did not have a good relationship and could never agree on the best way to resolve the pre-mix issue. Sometimes this perception of arrogance on the part of our DCE's was extended to our MP's. The classic example of such Ministers was Honourable Stephen Asamoah Boateng who was acknowledged by even his enemies to be hardworking but considered by even some admirers to be arrogant. He capped this by telling a caller on a radio show to be "careful because you are talking to a Minister of State". After a valiant effort, he lost his seat.

RUNNING MATE POLITICS

One of the significant events during the year was the choice of running mates. There were disruptive noises in both the NPP and NDC during the choice of their running mates. On the NDC side, former President Rawlings and the former first lady appeared to be unhappy at the choice of John Mahama. The former first lady said that in her view, Mr. Mahama was not competent. It appears though that in the end, most people considered John Mahama a solid choice. An additional benefit to Professor Mills was that his choice in the face of opposition from the former President and his wife helped Mills to reclaim some of his credentials as "his own man".

On the NPP side, the public nature of the campaign for running mate, da Rocha's virtual veto of the choice of Hajia Alima Mahama and the confusion that surrounded the surprise choice of Dr. Bawumia were not helpful to the ticket. Of note, the NPP tickets for the Presidency have generally been more balanced than the NDC. Since the return to democracy, the NDC has had South-South as well as all-Christian tickets but the NPP has always had North-South and Christian-Muslim tickets. Thus on the evidence, our tickets have been more inclusive.

VIOLENCE IN TAMALE

When the NPP running-mate visited Tamale after his selection, there was an outbreak of violence. In response, the NPP Chairman Mac Manu, addressed the Press and called for calm. However, in October as the situation continued to worsen, we had another conference addressed by Campaign Chairman, Jake Obetsebi-Lamptey. This followed a meeting during which our leadership pledged to do our part to pull the country from the brink of violence. Throughout the campaign, the NPP were very conscious of our responsibility to ensure peace because we were in government. Indeed, a few days after addressing the media, Mr. Mac Manu wrote a historic letter to the NDC Chairman, Dr. Kwabena Adjei, calling for joint action to curb the violence. In his October 24th address, Jake pledged his party once more to work for a peaceful election. He concluded "To opinion leaders and stake-holders, we urge forthright denunciation of the purveyors of violence. On our part, we shall, as we have done throughout this campaign, continue to work for peace. We believe that violence has no place in our politics. We shall continue our campaign of ideas and continue to avoid insults.

We shall continue to urge restraint on the part of our supporters.

We shall co-operate fully with the security forces to ensure peace.

As we move towards election-day, we urge the media to work with us to create an atmosphere of peace , calm, law and order. This they must do without fear or favour to any side. They must return to the higher ethics of their noble profession, calling things as they see them.

Let us move forward.

Let us reject violence and those who forment it.

Let us have a peaceful election.

Let us be an example to Kenya, Zimbabwe and their likes, not their imitators."

VISIT TO NORTH AMERICA

In the first half of June, the campaign visited North America. We visited Toronto, New York, Chicago, Washington D.C., Los Angeles and Atlanta. With the exception of the Atlanta event that the candidate could not attend, he attended all the other events, which were very well patronized.. The best organized of the events were the ones in Toronto and New York. One mishap that really upset the New Yorkers was when the General Secretary, Nana Ohene Ntow, berated the North American executives publicly for describing themselves as "National" executives. He took serious exception to the fact that the Chairman and General Secretary respectively for the US branch of the party are referred to as National Chairman and General Secretary. As he put it, "The NPP has only one National Chairman and one General Secretary and people here should stop referring to themselves by those titles".

That public rebuke was in very bad taste and upset quite a few people. The NPP North America Chair, Kofi Boateng and his team, worked very hard to co-ordinate the whole trip. Chairman Boateng criss-crossed the country to be with us wherever we went. The local leaders too, were wonderful. Mc Donald Agbenyo and Fred Bonsu in Toronto, Steve Mallory and Dr. Akyeampong in New York, Kofi Amoabeng and Dr. Ohemeng in Chicago, Nyarko and Mohammed Idris in Washington with Ambassador Adusei in the background, Dr. Adutwum and others in Los Angeles as well as Kwasi Agyemang and Sam Nyarko in Atlanta and their respective teams, all put in a lot of work. Historically, many in the Diaspora have felt under-appreciated by the party at home. They complained frequently that people want them to just bring resources and keep quiet. On the other hand, many at home think too often, their brothers and sisters abroad "talk too much and do too little". This writer was told by quite a few people that this view on the home front was reinforced when in 1996, a group of Diasporans persuaded the party at home to form an alliance with the CPP that made incumbent Vice-President Kow Nkensen Arkaah the running-mate of President Kufuor. It is claimed that one of the most persuasive arguments made by Dr George Ayittey of Washington D.C. and Dr. Agyenim Boateng of the Commonwealth of Kentucky was that the "Diasporans" would significantly increase their contributions if there was such an alliance. Unfortunately, when the alliance occurred the contributions did not come in as expected.

Sometimes, some in the Diaspora have difficulty understanding some of the decisions made in the heat of the campaign. For instance, some of the diasporans felt the North American trip was not planned well enough and that more places in the Diaspora should have been visited. Back home, most people felt that in the absence of ROPAL, spending two weeks in North America was unnecessary.

FAITH AND POLITICS

The role of religious people in campaigns is one area that is shrouded in mystery. The pervasive presence of people of faith was underlined recently when President Mills told a group of Pentecostals that he hoped they would turn the whole of Ghana into a prayer camp.

During the NPP primary, I remembered visiting a constituency in the Northern Region with my team. When we were about to leave, a distinguished-looking man with white beard described by his followers as a mallam, who was a constituency executive approached us. He said he had seen a vision of my success and been directed to sacrifice on my behalf. He further indicated that he had bought sheep and slaughtered it on his own for my safety and protection on the road. He told us the price of the sacrifice and we ended up paying for it. Later we realized that we had fallen for the oldest trick in the book.

Virtually every candidate had religious people praying for him.

While sometimes, the initiative was from the candidate and while the religious people were genuine men and women of God, there were some strange occurrences. Some approached the campaign with predictions of victory and demanded access to the candidate to perform rituals that would fortify the candidate. Others fasted and prayed. Personally, during the NPP primaries, some of my friends started a prayer group for me that met by conference monthly. It was very ably co-ordinated by Dr George Acquaah-Mensah of Boston, Massachusetts and Christian Dadzie, a Church of Pentecost elder, here in Ghana. Each meeting was led by a designated person. There was singing and prayers, asking for Gods blessing for our enterprise and for God's will to be done.

In the end, some even said the difference was made by Evangelist T.D. Joshua with whom Professor Mills worships. I do not know if there is any substance to this belief but I hope that some day, some who are more knowledgeable can shed some light on the relationship between campaigning and people of faith.

Before the first round, I did not hear any predictions of a second round. However, once there was a second round, a lot of prophets claimed to have predicted that in advance. After the elections, I heard President Mills say at a thanksgiving service that the Prophet had told him that they would be three votes, the first round, the second round and that of TAIN and that the winner would not be known till January. That would be the first verified, accurate prediction that I heard.

In addition to those who wanted to pray for candidates, there is an overtly religious tone to our political rallies that is fascinating. Virtually every party has prayers before and after gatherings. In the NPP, no party meeting gets underway without a prayer or closes without one. Towards the end, I was privileged to work with Hon. S.K. Boafo, in an effort to reach out to the religious community. As an ordained Minister, he brought to that effort a superb knowledge of the faith community.

The widespread involvement of religious people in our politics is a good thing. If the earnestness with which people in politics pray is manifested all throughout our political activity, it will be good for our politics and our nation.

RALLIES

One of the biggest events in the campaign was the Kasoa rally. While it was probably the biggest rally of the campaign, it lulled too many of us into attaching too much importance to rallies.

Throughout the campaign, many kept referring to the attendance at our rallies as proof that we were going to do well. I kept noticing that the NDC rallies were also very well attended. As some veterans of past campaigns kept reminding everyone, the NPP had held some of the biggest rallies in our history on our way to defeat in 1992.

Another issue that plagued us throughout the campaign was misinformation. Every region's party leaders were sure that we were going to do very well in their region. This kind of blind optimism made it very difficult to make realistic estimates of our strengths and to predict our performance.

Based on this optimism, they demanded more resources even in situations where the chances were hopeless and thus deprived viable and winnable areas of the vital resources needed to win. For example, right till the end, Central Regional party leaders were insisting that we could win a majority of the popular vote in the Presidential election in the region and all nineteen Parliamentary seats.

With two weeks to go for the poll, the campaign team met to review our expectations. Buoyed by polls that suggested a first round victory and a Parliamentary majority, we felt confident.

Even then, the predictions appeared too optimistic to me and I said so. The Central Region team was still predicting 17 seats for us. When I asked Alhaji Gibrine, the Regional Organizer, who was seated next to me if he believed those predictions, he said no but he did not want to disagree with the Chair of his team in public. He told me the team had not done their own constituency by constituency analysis before coming to our meeting.

CHAPTER ELEVEN
LOSING ROUND ONE

"About 30% of African elections come down to ways and means on election day"

Anonymous African Election Official

DIVISIONS

Up till the end, Constituency campaign teams were hampered in many instances, by unnecessary divisions. For instance, in the Cape Coast constituency, repeated meetings were held to improve relationships between the Parliamentary candidate, Amponsah-Dadzie and those opposed to him. There were complaints that the candidate was absent from the constituency too often and seemed determined not to work with his erstwhile opponents. Party elders complained of not being involved in things. I remember being invited to a meeting that lasted over three hours and focused entirely on healing our divisions instead of how to defeat the NDC. In the end, even though we agreed on how everyone could work together, that meeting had the feel of defeat all over it. The meeting was attended by the Parliamentary candidate, the Constituency Chairman, Mr. Hutchful and elders Nana Awuku, Kojo Mensah Alata and Mrs. Adu Boahen. It was painful hearing the elders invoke the greatness of the party in the past and the need for unity. In the end, we lost Cape Coast.

The divisions described for Cape Coast where also present in many other constituencies. Amongst these were Abura-Asebu-Kwamankese, Agona-Enyan-Essiam, Yendi, Salaga, Navrongo, Ablekuma-South, Nkawkaw and many others.

ELECTION-DAY ACTIVITIES

Right from the beginning, it was agreed that election day activities would be crucial to winning the elections.

Amongst these were mobilizing our voters, policing the voting, ensuring fair counting and making sure the entire process was secure.

Preparation for voting day started long before the actual day. Throughout the year, there were persistent rumours that the NDC had an elaborate plan to compromise the Electoral Commission and the voting process. Even while we worked to prevent these rumours from being realised, the NDC kept accusing us of being in cahoots with the Electoral Commission to rig the vote.

The first major issue that came up was the Voters' Registration. While we worked hard to get our people registered, we worried about the NDC trying to register aliens and under-aged voters. There were reports of busloads of people being brought into the country from neighbouring countries to register. Many people came forward with plans to help foil these illegal and/or inappropriate registrations. To be fair, not all those from outside a constituency coming to register were foreigners or under-aged voters .Many were people who hailed from the constituency but were domiciled elsewhere coming back home to register. Also, according to sources in the Electoral Commission, quite a few were people trying to replace lost cards who were unsure about the procedure.

In general and consistent with their general optimism, local party leaders assured us that our people were registering.

There were accusations and counter-accusations about malpractices that in some instances, led to violence.

HIRING OF RETURNING OFFICERS

The next issue was recruiting Returning Officers. Right from day one, our goal was to make sure that those hired were not hostile to our interests. This involved working with our local party leaders to encourage those who had served as Returning Officers before and were fair to us to apply and protesting against the hiring of those perceived to be sympathizers of the NDC or hostile to our interests. Most of these Returning Officers were teachers. In the end, there were many complaints by NPP party leaders that those hired were generally sympathetic to the NDC. As Dan Botwe, who was in charge explained, the fact that local party leaders think a particular Returning Officer is not known as a sympathizer does not make the person a bad Returning Officer. He said many of those who were the target of protests had been identified by others as very fair Returning Officers. Despite Dan's explanation, it appeared that the general feeling around the campaign was that we had lost the battle with regards to Returning Officers. This writer too, was subject to the same accusations when the NPP had to list the order of Preference for Debate moderators. The same moderator could be described as very friendly and very hostile by two very respected NPP members. Thus when the Opportunity was offered to challenge some of them, it was difficult to know whom to challenge.

POLLING AGENTS

The next task was to select and train polling agents for election day.

Right from day one, it was decided that these agents would be selected mainly from TERTIARY EDUCATION CONFEDERACY OF THE NEW PATROITIC PARTY (TESCON) members who would be paid for their services and trained ahead of time.

The selection of mainly Tescon members would later come back to haunt us. The campaign, under the leadership of Dan Botwe trained them all around the country in the "dos" and "donts" of being a polling agent.

A few days before the vote, I was asked by Dr. Apraku to join him and others in a "PRESS CONFERENCE" to warn the country about the rigging plans of the NDC. The Campaign Director said that people we had successfully infiltrated into the NDC campaign had reported that the NDC had procured large quantities of indelible ink with which they planned to spoil ballots in NPP strongholds. He displayed some of the ink and recounted how, according to our agents, the NDC planned to use the ink. Afterwards some of us held anguished discussions about what the Electoral Commission and the Security Agencies were doing to prevent any Electioneering malpractices. Dr. Apraku said representation had been made to the Security Agencies and that he had assurances that the vote would be secure. Later, it turned out that the NPP had lost the vote in most of the barracks. Indeed, some soldiers had gone to the polls saying that "Sergeant Agya Atta should go". While there is no evidence of wrong-doing, this may explain the peculiar situation of a governing party complaining impotently about rigging by the opposition party.

VOTING DAY SUPPORT

On voting day, many of these agents complained that they did not get the needed support from party and constituency leaders. Some also claimed they had not been paid their allowances. Even some complained that those tasked with supplying them with food had either not shown up at all or shown up late. Indeed, a lot of the rice that was supposed to be transported all over the country was inexplicably still in warehouses in Accra on voting day. The campaign team had been unable to transport them to where they were needed.

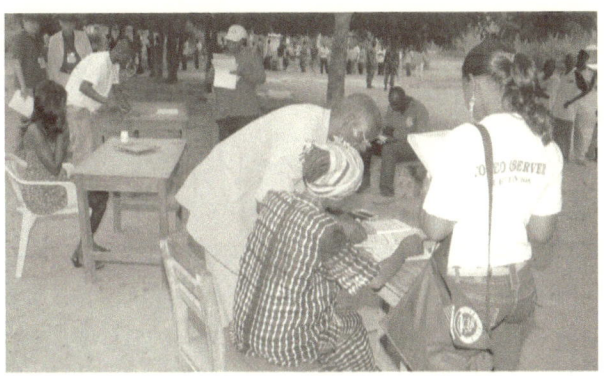

Voting day, Dec. 7th, 2008

In 2000, volunteers supplied our polling agents with so much food that there was excess that was passed on to other party agents. Later on, some of these parties, notably the NDC would complain that their agents had been given contaminated food that had made them sick.

In the event, this led to very low morale and lapses in performance. There were reports of agents leaving to go and find food and of others reading as the voting took place. There were very heroic polling agents though. Some, outnumbered in NDC strongholds, called for re-enforcement in vain while their party leaders were nowhere to be found. Some recounted stories of trying to follow ballot boxes to collating centres with their own money.

In Kumasi, while polling agents looked for party leaders to help resolve problems, one party leader was reportedly holed up at his girlfriend's place.

One area where we made elaborate plans was that of transporting party supporters to vote in places where they had registered. There was a lot of planning but the day before voting, there was widespread chaos as party members queued up for buses whose numbers turned out to be inadequate. At the University of Cape Coast, many who resided elsewhere but needed to vote there had difficulty getting there to vote. It appeared that many who had transferred their votes had problems identifying places to vote and solving other logistical problems. Some believe that this may have affected our party's chances in the Cape Coast constituency.

As counting got underway, there were reports that some of our people were not up to the task.

Despite their training, too many did not appear to have a clear grasp of the intricacies of counting and collating results.

VOTING IRREGULARITIES

Clear examples are Ayawaso Central and Weija, the constituencies of Honourables I.C. Quaye and Ayorkor Botchway, respectively, where recounts led to significant increases in NPP votes. Many in the NPP also believe that the Asutifi South seat won by Collins Dauda was won by chicanery achieved through a superior ground operation.

Before the voting, Parliamentary candidates were also trained by a team led by the National Chairman, and including Brigadier Odei. The Parliamentary candidates were given guidance on how to form and manage their campaign teams. Most of these training sessions were poorly attended. The sessions drummed home the need for inclusiveness, accountability and humility. Later, there were stories of candidates who did not know their polling agents or failed to visit their collation centers. Also, there were reports of Parliamentary candidates who having won their seats, seemed uninterested in the presidential poll.

The last part was keeping a record of the votes in Accra. In 2000, the NPP's collation was always ahead of the Electoral Commission by hours and most radio stations announced results released by the NPP before EC results became public.

PROPHECIES OF DEFEAT

About two months before the vote, I met Ben Ephson, the renowned pollster and political strategist in Cape Coast. When I asked him, as a strategist what he thought would determine the elections, he was very prophetic. He said" I think the NPP has three problems in this election. The problems are Central Region, Greater Accra and Ashanti. In Central and Greater Accra, you are trailing and need more support. In Ashanti, your problem is apathy. They support you but not enough will vote. My pollsters are picking up historic levels of apathy. It suggests that you need a major turnout operation to get your supporters in Ashanti to the polls." Within the campaign, some publicity experts, particularly Geddy Laryea had been warning us against the "AGBENA CAMPAIGN". Geddy warned repeatedly that in an election that was this close, the sense of complacency projected by that campaign could cost us crucial votes, from voters who would stay home in the belief that the elections was already won.

About a couple of weeks before the vote, Bede Zeiding of the Democratic Freedom Party visited our office. In a masterful presentation, right in the corridor, the former NDC operative analysed the Northern Region, constituency by constituency. When he predicted that he expected Alhaji Malik Yakubu, Boniface Siddique, Charles Bintim and Hajia Alima Mahama to lose, someone openly burst into laughter and asked whether he was sane. While most in the office that day were too busy to listen, I listened as he gave me a masterful presentation about the politics of the region, pointing out where ethnicity mattered and where religion mattered, his passion rising as the sweat soaked his shirt.

On election night, as the mighty fell, I remembered Bede, standing in that corridor and predicting the nightmare that was to come for us in the north.

On voting day, I voted at Asebu in the Abora-Asebu-Kwamankese constituency. On my way back to Accra, I made stops at a number of polling stations, including some at University Of Cape Coast. There I learned of complaints about transfers not going through and difficulties with transport for those trying to get to their voting places. I called the campaign headquarters and relayed the concerns expressed in Cape Coast. In Accra, I found that some complaints had been coming in but that campaign leaders still expected us to win. Indeed, when voting closed, we called around for reports and then retired for the evening.

That night, a National Executive member was spotted having dinner at a hotel in Accra by a shocked diplomat. I got home after midnight but could not get to sleep. Before we retired, there were wildly optimistic results from the North in general and the Northern Region in particular. It seemed we were on our way to making historic breakthroughs in the Northern region. When the dust finally settled, most of the hype was not borne out. In the early hours of the morning, my phone rang and it was the Chief of Staff, Mr. Kojo Mpiani. He informed me that Koku Anyidoho had just issued a statement alleging that the polls were being rigged for the NPP and advised that we needed to respond immediately. I drove back to the office and together with Jake Obetsebi Lamptey, discussed the outline of a statement that was later read to the media. By evening a lot of the results were in and as the two parties battled in the media to reassure their supporters, something became apparent. Despite the many discussions on the collation of results, it appeared that our system for getting results was not up to the standards of previous elections. At some point, it seemed that the Campaign Director and the National Chairman had different results for some constituencies. Looking for good numbers, I went to Dr. Wireko Brobbey's office. It seemed his collation centre was quieter and had more serious and professional staff. Around midnight, I went back for an update on results and met the Chief Of Staff.

After some discussions, we compared results and realized that Joy FM and Dr. Wireko Brobbey's centre both had a handful of constituencies left. On comparing the list, we quickly figured out which constituencies were missing from Dr. Wireko-Brobbey's list. He sent me into the next room to get the missing numbers from Dr. Wireko Brobbey. With the Chief of Staff holding a pen and paper and Dr. Wireko Brobbey calling out the numbers, we figured out that we would be short of a first-round victory by about 65 thousand. In the early hours of the morning, while the nation waited, the Chief of Staff and I paid Nana Akufo-Addo a visit at his office, a few minutes walk away. When the NPP candidate learned that he would be unable to win "one-touch", he was disappointed but not discouraged.

Throughout the campaign, while the presidential elections were seen to be close, many assumed that the Parliamentary contest would be won decisively by us.

Thus while our inability to win the presidential election in the first round was a surprise, the loss of our Parliamentary majority was a shock.

From north to south and east to west, members of parliament considered well entrenched had gone down to defeat.

Amongst the defeated MP's were two former vice-presidential candidates and quite a number of Ministers.

CHAPTER TWELVE
LOSING ROUND TWO

"When you fail to plan, you plan to fail"

Anonymous

REACTIONS TO FIRST ROUND RESULTS

WHEN WE REALIZED THERE WAS GOING to be a second round, the NPP was stunned and the NDC was ecstatic. Throughout the campaign, on the basis of the "Agbena Campaign", the NPP had never planned for a second round. Indeed, once, when I asked a very senior member of the campaign what would be our strategy for a second round, he said confidently and incredulously "There is not going to be any second round." On the other hand, the NDC had always campaigned on the assumption that there would be a second round. For instance, during the campaign, I had been asked to explore the possibility of arranging a one-on-one debate between Nana Akufo-Addo and Professor Mills. When I broached the topic with my NDC contact he said the NDC would not be interested because, "we don't want to offend the small parties. When there is a second round, we think we are going to need their help." I remember meeting Hon. Haruna Idrisu right after the first round. He was ecstatic that there was going to be a second round and giddy about the NDC performance in the Parliamentary election.

SECOND ROUND STRATEGY

The first time Jake Obetsebi Lamptey, I and strategist Larry Gibson held a discussion of the second round was on the morning after the first round vote. At that point, our figures showed Nana Akufo-Addo had a lead that was diminishing by the moment. Obviously, it is possible that others in the campaign had discussed this in my absence but if so, I had not been informed.

Mr. Larry Gibson recommended that since this was a "radio nation", we put more emphasis on radio interviews and advertising during the second round.

The morning after the results were announced, the Campaign Director convened a meeting.

As soon as the meeting was called to order, the presidential candidate started with some remarks.

He said he was making some major changes.

First, he was taking personal control of the entire campaign. Secondly he, wanted the National Chairman, Peter Mac Manu, to be the Field Director with day-to-day operational control of the campaign, assisted by Kwabena Agyapong. Third, he wanted Jake Obetsebi Lamptey to be in charge of advertising and media relations, to be assisted by Madam Oboshie Sai Cofie.

In addition, he also wanted changes made in some regions where the campaigns needed more punch. Amongst these regions were Western, Central and Ashanti regions.

He wanted Nana Owusu Ankomah replaced as Western Region Campaign Chair by his brother, Papa Owusu Ankomah. Dr. Heyman was to take over the Central Region team from Hon. Kennedy Agyapong while Alan Kyerematen was to take over Ashanti from Kan Dapaah with Osafo Maafo taking over Eastern Region.

Then he opened the floor for comments. Unfortunately, while others had a lot to say, Nana Akufo-Addo's remarks had made most of the comments moot. Generally, it would have been preferable to have people discuss their views of why we lost. Then based on these views, we should have looked at changes. Lord Commey objected to being excluded from Field Operations. "It is wrong to exclude the National Organizer from this and I want to put this on record." Nana Akufo-Addo responded that he had taken account of Lord's comments but "since it is my Presidency that is at stake, I am taking responsibility."

Within days of this meeting, the President convened another meeting in his house to convey his concerns and his recommendations to the campaign hierarchy. While I was not present at that meeting, I was told that it was a very effective meeting. Within a day, we learned that Alan Kyerematen had declined to take charge of Ashanti because some in the region had raised objections. As soon as the meeting was over, I went to Jake Obetsebi Lamptey and told him that in view of the changes made, I wanted to go back to the Central Region and help. "No, you are not going anywhere. You are going to be right here to help me run this." Within hours, Jake Obetsebi Lamptey, Oboshie and I had a meeting at which it was decided that I should join Nana Akufo-Addo on the road to help emphasize the priorities of the communication team on the road. For the second round, we were going to make the candidate more accessible to the media. Now wherever we went, we visited a radio station for an interview before going to talk to the gathered crowds. We would drive to the station and Nana Akufo-Addo would take questions for about half-an-hour before any other activity. At Bibiani, for instance, we got to the station just before midnight and had the interview anyway.

After that meeting, I did not see Peter Mac Manu till the night of the elections.

ON THE ROAD WITH NANA

On the road, we first headed for Central Region and to Winneba. Due to our performance on the coast, we wanted to reach out to fishermen. Therefore, we arranged an event on the beach with fishermen, to be preceded by a walking visit to fishermen by their boats. When we rounded a corner, we came upon four young fishermen, squatting by their boat and eating a lunch of gari, pepper and fish. Nana Akufo-Addo stopped to chat for a few minutes. The idea was to have the candidate interact alone with the fishermen. Unfortunately, once the event started, things got out of hand. All manner of people who were not involved or not expected showed up and wanted to speak.

That was where the famous begging incident by Christine Churcher occurred. Right in the middle of her speech, she dropped to her needs and started begging for forgiveness. It was quite a performance. In the next few days, all the nation would hear about was the NPP begging for forgiveness. As the NDC stated pointedly, "Ask them what sins they are begging your forgiveness for." Then we headed to Mankessim and to Cape Coast and other places. That evening, he was interviewed by the Ghana Broadcasting Corporation (GBC) in Cape Coast.

In addition to the visits, we stepped up advertising. Even while on the road, we took advantage every break in the candidate's schedule to record radio and television adverts. Also, we fought very hard to get the pictures to Accra.

Every morning, I would call Accra or receive a call from either Jake Obetsebi Lamptey or Oboshie and they would give me guidance of themes to emphasise and to bring up. Also, I had a very easy relationship with Nana Akufo-Addo and we discussed ideas back and forth. After each interview, he would ask how it had gone and we would discuss how to refine his answers for subsequent interviews.

ROLE OF PARLIAMENTARY CANDIDATES IN THE SECOND ROUND

One group whose role was very interesting was the Parliamentary candidates. Regardless of the results, some just disappeared for the second round.

On the night of the first round, Nana Ato Arthur, for instance was very concerned and called frequently for updates. So too, did Honourable. Abraham Odum, of Twifu-Atimokwa.

During the second round, in Central Region, Asabe and Odum, amongst the defeated candidates, were perhaps the most active. I remember visiting Odum at Twifu-Praso. I got there around nine that night and he was just finishing his last rally. These two toured their constituencies repeatedly and urged the voters who had just rejected them to vote for Nana Akufo-Addo while many others just started to follow the candidate or to lick their wounds in private. In Ashanti while he had not been very active in the first round, Dr Richard Anane was reported to have worked very hard.

THE SMALLER PARTIES IN THE SECOND ROUND

Once the second round was announced, the leanings of the smaller parties became very important. Efforts were made at the level of the candidate to engage them immediately. It was felt that we could count on Dr. Nduom and Alhaji Ramadan to help swing the CPP behind us. Dr. Nduom had served in the Kufuor administration while Alhaji Ramadan was the father-in-law of the NPP running-mate, Dr. Mamudu Bawumia.

On the PNC side, Dr. Mahama, we believed was at heart one of us. In 2000, he had been offered the NPP running-mate slot and had reportedly turned it down. Unfortunately, both parties were unable to get their National Executives to endorse the NPP. At heated meetings, both parties were unable to muster clear majorities in support of either party. However, on the ground, it soon became evident that operatives of the two parties were working for the NDC in most constituencies.

Within a few hours after the results were announced, I learned that Nana Akufo-Addo had contacted Dr. Nduom. While we were in Kumasi, the two exchanged phone calls and my impression from Nana Akufo-Addo was that Dr. Nduom would be supportive. We heard that he was on his way to Ho to campaign for us. When he finally got there, Dr. Nduom talked of "NDUOM FOR 2012". I was also informed that contact had been made with Dr. Edward Mahama and other PNC leaders.

Later on, Dr Nduom reportedly told a close friend that "I got more calls from the President urging me to support the NPP than from the candidate."

The DFP released a very good statement endorsing the NPP Candidate for the second round, signed by Bede Zeding. Around the same time, Mr. Obed Asamoah made very supportive remarks during an interview.

ISSUES FOR SECOND ROUND

Two factors that became very significant were the Parliamentary results as well as the spread of the voting across the regions.

When the results showed the NDC ahead of the count with 114 seats, they started claiming that they had won the Parliamentary majority and that if they did not win the Presidential vote, the country would be ungovernable. This argument seemed to carry weight with a lot of people and in stop after stop, the NPP candidate had to patiently explain how we could mathematically end up with the majority in Parliament. In our haste to cobble together a Parliamentary majority, we forgot our pre-election vow to punish the independents and started courting them. In addition, we reminded people of all the places where the results were challenged, like Akwatia, Asutifi South and Sefwi-Wiawso.

The claim by the NDC that they had won seven regions also made our supporters uneasy despite the fact that the results had nothing to do with the number of regions that were won.

As the NDC pointed these things out, we also made the case, quite vociferously that the nation, contrary to what the NDC was claiming had not voted for change. We reminded voters that in 2000, after the first round, the change candidate, the NPP's John Agyekum Kufuor had been ahead. Furthermore, we pointed out that Nana Akufo-Addo was much further ahead than President Kufuor was after the first round in 2000.

Perhaps, in addition to the ill-advised apologies, the most damaging thing we did was the reduction of petrol prices and the release of incarcerated drivers before the second round. It gave voters the unfortunate impression that we could have eased the difficulties of their lives but had failed to do so and were only doing so belatedly to get votes.

On election day, I voted once again at my hometown, Asebu, in the Abura-Asebu-Kwamankese constituency and on my way back to Accra, stopped in Cape Coast. At the University, I found the lines shorter than they were and the same problems that existed during the first round were there. The only difference was that they had gotten worse.

Early on election-day we started getting reports that our polling agents were being molested in the Volta Region. Later, it was revealed that these incidents had started the day before with the beating of gong and public announcements in some communities urging the people of the Volta Region to "resist the foreigners who had come to take over our voting process." That day in town after town, polling agents under assault had taken refuge in police stations or fled the towns where they had been sent as polling agents. The most well-known of these cases was perhaps that of Dr. Sammy Ohene, a psychiatrist who was pushed by the police into the hands of a mob who assaulted him.

The NPP held a hastily convened Press Conference urging the Electoral Commission to suspend the voting in the Volta Region. The Commission did not act.

In addition to the Volta Region, in Greater Accra and Ashanti, throughout the day, there were episodic reports of ballot-box snatching incidents. Most of these were attributed to NDC activists and seem to fit into the pre-election warnings of violen

COMPLAINTS ABOUT VOTING

On the morning of the 2nd January, the EC Chair, Dr. Afari-Gyan announced that the results available showed that while Prof. Mills was ahead, it would be impossible to declare a winner without the votes of the Tain constituency. Therefore, he announced that Tain would vote on the 5th of January, 2009. In addition to that the EC Chair said the both the NPP and the NDC had complained about irregularities. The NDC complaints were about Ashanti while the NPP complaints were about the Volta Region. He added that he had asked both parties to present available evidence to his office since "the name of the game is evidence".

The NDC complaints were to do with vote tallies that were reportedly changed after being received in the Electoral Commission office. The EC Chair said the only votes deemed accepted were those with his signatures and he asked the NDC to provide the said results with his signature. They could not.

The NPP complaints concerned nearly three hundred thousand votes in the southern part of the Volta Region which we were disputing since our agents had been prevented from representing the interests of the NPP and its candidate, Nana Akufo-Addo. From the point of view of the campaign, we needed to get this evidence to the EC Chair early enough to make Tain irrelevant.

However, for reasons that were difficult to determine, the evidence did not get to the EC Chair that day and by the time it was ready, it had been changed from a protest addressed to the EC Chair to a petition aimed at restraining the EC Chair from holding the Tain Election. Apparently, the night the Tain elections were announced, a group of NPP lawyers had met for hours and in the end, with the exception of one of them, they concluded that there was no legal basis for stopping the elections in Tain. Despite this consensus from the group, it was decided to proceed with the case. It was filed by Hon. Atta Akyea and later withdrawn for being filed inappropriately.

Essentially, the crux of our case was that the NDC and others acting in its name had conspired to deprive the NPP and its Presidential candidate of their rights under the laws of Ghana by systematically preventing his designated agents from acting as polling agents and thus protecting his interests as a candidate. While the EC Chair and others conceded that there may have been irregularities, for purposes of electioneering, one needed specific types of evidence. One needed to show at polling station level that for instance more people had voted than were registered at that polling station to vote or systematic tampering with the votes in a manner that made it impossible to determine the will of the people. In other words, while preventing your agent from serving as a polling agent through assault might be a criminal offence, that on its own might not be sufficient to invalidate the results from that polling station. In other words, the very people who would have been our best witnesses were the agents who were bullied and chased out of the polling stations and SINCE WE DID NOT ACT TO PREVENT IT, THERE WAS NOTHING THAT COULD BE DONE ABOUT IT. By the time it became obvious that the court case would not fly, our failure to engage TAIN in the first two days had made it difficult to be competitive in TAIN.

CHAPTER THIRTEEN
LOSING TAIN IN ACCRA

"Tomorrow, there will be no vote in TAIN"

President Kufuor, at the Palace of the Omanhene of Wenchi

WITH THE MENTION OF "TAIN", THE parties started to scramble. Tain had been excluded from the elections on account of the destruction of the Electoral Commission office by arsonists. Many had assumed that the elections would be decided without the need for Tain.

When we spoke to the Brong-Ahafo Regional Chairman of the NPP, Adu Gyan, about Tain, he was not very optimistic. During the Parliamentary elections, there had been a very bitter primary involving incumbent NPP Member of Parliament Joe Danquah and the chiefs of the area. The chiefs did not want Mr. Danquah and accused him of being disrespectful and arrogant. Even though he was the incumbent, many were determined to oust him. Before the elections, a number of missions were sent to Tain by the NPP flag-bearer to resolve these misunderstandings. The last one had been led by Boakye Agyarko. Unfortunately, the misunderstandings could not be resolved.

Tain is a very big, rural constituency with communities widely spread out and connected by very bad roads.

As soon as the Electoral Commission made his announcement, NDC operatives, headed by former President Rawlings, headed for Tain. On the other hand, some NPP operatives also headed there. Soon we started getting reports that they were being harassed and that even the security agencies there were exhibiting bias towards the NDC. There were reports of soldiers openly exhibiting the "Yere Sesamu" sign of the NDC. Our operatives reported that they were being searched while NDC members were being allowed to go through freely without being searched.

As these reports kept coming, the NPP leadership was focused on how to resolve the problem through the courts. Without a firm commitment to contest the Tain election, our members on the ground were sensing the initiative and the energy shift to the NDC while they waited for direction and leadership.

PRESIDENT KUFUOR PLEDGES "NO VOTE"

The day before the vote, when I got to Wenchi on my way to Tain, I learned that both the President and the NPP Presidential candidate were in town. While the rest of us waited outside, the two leaders met to discuss the situation. I joined the delegation as they visited the traditional leaders in the area.

At the palace of the Omanhene, Nana Kwadwo Abrefa Nketia, the President said that due to the circumstances pertaining in Tain, "there is going to be no vote in Tain". This, coupled with the President's decision not to go to Tain because he reportedly did not want to exacerbate tensions, gave many the impression that the Tain election would be cancelled on the grounds of security.

Unfortunately, despite the President's statement, no concrete subsequent steps were taken. Throughout the afternoon, many people just waited in Tain or its environs, waiting to hear an official announcement that the elections had been cancelled.

In the event, no announcement came and voting took place the next day.

In retrospect, Tain was mishandled by the NPP. Even while fighting the election results in the courts, the Party and the campaign outfit should have been taking steps to contest the elections in Tain. Our supporters should have been given a chance to go down fighting instead of just giving away Tain the way we did.

The manner in which Tain was handled looked particularly bad since we were the party in government. As in our complaints about the maltreatment of our agents in the Volta Region, many in Ghana and around the world were unsympathetic to our complaints. They felt it was our responsibility to ensure security rather than complaining about the lack of security. Many felt that since we were in control of the security apparatus, we should have beefed up security instead of having press conferences about those who intended to cause violence.

Many questions will be asked for years about TAIN. Here are a few of those questions.

Why could the President not go to TAIN? If it was not safe for him to go, why could the vote take place?

Why did the NPP Candidate not go to TAIN?

Why did President Kufuor announce at Wenchi that there would be no vote in TAIN when he did not know that for a fact?

Why did the party that wrestled power from the NDC in 2000 allow power to be wrestled from them despite having the security forces under its control?

CHAPTER FOURTEEN
THE SMALL PARTIES

"Last week, someone walked up to me in a bank and thanked me
for the balance the small parties are providing. He urged us not to
be discouraged and assured me that our country and our democracy
needs us"

Bede Zeding, DFP General Secretary, in 2009

HISTORIC ALLIANCES

WHILE THERE IS NO DISPUTE ABOUT the dominance of our politics by
the NPP and the NDC, there is a lot of speculation about the strength
and influence of the small parties.

In 1996, the NPP had formed an alliance with the CPP, and as a
result picked incumbent Vice-President K.N. Arkaah as the running
mate for Mr. J.A. Kufuor. While the ticket went down to defeat,
the NPP had continued its alliance with most of the smaller parties.
Indeed, before the 2000 elections, the PNC's Dr. Mahama was offered
the chance to be Mr. Kufuor's running mate but turned it down.

However, there was no doubt that the small parties shared fully the
NPP's desire for change.

During the elections, the NPP had entered into alliances with other parties in various constituencies. In the Komenda-Edina-Eguafo-Abirem constituency, Dr. Nduom had been supported by the NPP which had not fielded any candidate. This same arrangements had been repeated in the Nzema constituencies where Freddie Blay and Kwesi Armah, both of the CPP had been supported. Thus, during the second round, the CPP and the PNC did not hesitate in supporting the NPP.

After the election, these alliances continued and were manifested in some members in these parties being appointed to key positions in the NPP government.

Dr. Nduom served throughout the NPP term in key ministerial positions while others, like Moses Dani-Baah, and Mallam Issah, also served in other positions. Indeed, in 2007, when NPP Ministers running for President were asked to resign, Dr. Nduom was allowed to stay much longer in the government before resigning. However, as time passed, while the individuals who had been appointed stayed close to the NPP, their parties drifted apart from the NPP.

HOW THE SMALLER PARTIES DRIFTED AWAY

Gradually, they found common cause with the NDC as they teamed up with them through the Committee for Joint Action (CJA). While in the past, NPP firebrands like Dr. Wireko-Brobbey and Nana Akufo-Addo had been natural leaders of the CJA and their protests, these positions were taken over by Kwasi Pratt, Omane Boama and Okudzeto Ablakwa, with Professor Mills joining in occasionally.

By 2008, during the Congresses of the small parties, the NDC seemed more welcoming than the NPP.

For example, at the PNC's annual congress last year, the NDC is reported to have made a donation while the NPP did not. Also, in 2008, the NPP, thinking it could go it alone, abandoned the alliances that had helped the small parties win seats in constituencies where they were strong,, in return for which they backed our Presidential candidate. Indeed, when in early 2008, NPP Chairman Mac Manu suggested broadening the alliance by opting out of about 15 seats to show goodwill to the smaller parties, he was overruled. As he put it then "We cannot win all the 230 seats. Some of these parties have very good chances of winning some of them and we should help them to win rather split the anti-NDC votes and thus help the NDC to win."

On the side of the small parties, the associations with the NPP were to have ripple effects that would affect the cohesion and unity of their parties during the 2008 elections.

THE CPP

In the CPP contest for flag-bearer, the two front-runners were both people who had held positions in the NPP government; Dr. Paa Kwesi Nduom and Dr.Agyemang Badu Akosa.

Dr. Nduom had held ministerial portfolios while Dr. Akosa had been the Director of the Ghana Health Service.

As they squared off against Dr. Kwaku Sarfo and others, there were questions of loyalty to the CPP and consistency with their underlying principle. Dr. Nduom, for instance, was accused of not supporting his party's Presidential candidate in 2004, Mr. Agudey.

At the Kwame Nkrumah University for Science and Technology (KNUST), where the CPP nominating congress was held, there were a lot of young delegates and a lot of energy. Talking to the delegates, it was obvious that the CPP was a divided party. Later, it appeared that Dr. Nduom may have won because the patriots may have divided their votes between Drs.Akosa and Kwaku Sarfo. Even though Dr. Nduom won, he had his work cut out for him. He needed to unite his party.

Early in the campaign, Dr. Nduom seemed to be getting a lot of attention and energizing the CPP on the ground. He reached his high-water mark with the first debate which most observers believed he had won. The "Chronicle" front page headline the day after said it all "TRANCENDENTAL NDUOM CONNECTS".

Unfortunately, right after that, the wheels started coming off of his campaign. In a public dispute, he was openly criticized by the CPP National Youth Organizer, Mr. Kwabena Bomfe, of running a non-inclusive campaign. The public row over Dr. Nduom's leadership style, in the home stretch of the campaign could not have come at a worse time.

NDUOM REFLECTS ON 2008

Reflecting on the campaign later, in 2009, to a group of students at the Harvard University's Kennedy School of Government, Dr. Nduom said " I need a team, loyal and trustworthy that will unite around our message and work hard on our common cause to win power".

On the issues that contributed to the CPP's defeat, according to the Daily Graphic of Thursday, April 16th "he mentioned the inability to raise required funds to inspire the ordinary people to support the his campaign, the inability of the CPP to field credible and resourceful Parliamentary candidates to lead the campaign at the local level and the lack of a united front in the rank and file of the party."

Elsewhere, Dr. Nduom added "But a very big challenge was the electorate, mostly poor, living in communities deprived of the basics; water, electricity, schools, housing, safe roads, good health facilities and faced with high unemployment and who were only willing to vote for the one they believe would give them what they want now. Unfortunately, they were material I could not afford to give."

From his special vantage point, Dr. Nduom's perspective deserves serious consideration. He does identify lack of financial resources as key to the failure of the CPP to do better. That appears very reasonable. He also identified lack of unity in his party and the quality of candidates. Uniting the party, one might suggest, is the primary responsibility of the party's Presidential candidate. That this did not occur does not reflect well on Dr. Nduom as leader of his party. It is possible that Dr. Nduom made efforts we are not aware of to unify his party but was unsuccessful. His inability to unify his party was the subject of the public comments by the CPP's National Youth Organizer, Mr. Kwabena Bomfe, as mentioned earlier. In addition to the factors raised by Mr. Bomfe, Dr. Nduom's public spats with Former Deputy Speaker Blay of Ellembelle constituency did not help. To be fair to Dr. Nduom, he might have added that due to the timing of the CPP primary, he did not have enough time.

The part of Dr. Nduom's reflection that should concern us is his implication that people voted in response to financial inducements. He compounds this by implying that if he had resources, he would have done the same. Even if his initial view about the influence of money on voting by ordinary people was supportable, he should have condemned the practice instead of wishing he had the resources to indulge in it. While Dr. Nduom's point on the influence of money applies significantly to primaries in all parties, its role in general elections is dubious. It is true that money is crucial to every political campaign. As former U.S. President Bill Clinton was fond of saying "Money is the mother's milk of politics". In general elections, however, parties and candidates who are outspent win often.

To make another credible run, Dr. Nduom must rebuild his bridges to his party and prevent the NDC from appropriating the symbols and history of his party. Indeed, in my judgment, the central tasks facing the CPP are the ability to get credible candidates on the ground, their ability to unite with the P.N.C. and the need to prevent the NDC from presenting itself as the inheritors of Nkrumah's legacy.

PEOPLES' NATIONAL CONVENTION

The PNC was essentially a creation of Dr Hilla Limann, the President of the third Republic. He created that to contest the 1992 elections and was badly beaten. The PNC, under Dr. Edward Mahama, appears to be stuck at 1%. They appear to have strength in sections of the Upper West, Upper East and Northern Region. This, until the last election, has always translated into Parliamentary seats.

Despite his obvious vision and integrity, Dr. Mahama has been the PNC's Presidential candidate a number of times without any discernible improvement in their performance. Before he was re-nominated as the PNC Presidential candidate, there were dissenting voices about his eligibility to contest the party's nomination based on their constitution. In the initial stages of the NPP government, there was collaboration between the PNC and the NPP. As a result of this collaboration, some PNC members were appointed to key positions.

It seems that whatever he chooses to do, Dr. Mahama has served his country very well----- in Medicine.

I think he missed his chance to have significant impact when in 2000 he turned down the chance to be the NPP's running-mate. I have no doubt that if he had accepted that offer, he could have helped shape our country significantly. As things stand now, the best thing for his party will be for Dr. Mahama to step aside in favour of new leadership.

THE DEMOCRATIC FREEDOM PARTY

The one new party that also had potential that was unrealized was the Democratic Freedom Party. Led by Mr. Obed Asamoah and created out of mostly former NDC members, the party got off to a flying start. Unfortunately, after speculations about the candidacy of Dr. Kwesi Botchway, the party ended up picking a Presidential candidate, Emmanuel Ansah-Antwi, who despite being a very fine man, was relatively unknown to the public. This made it difficult for the party to get traction during the elections.

As for the remaining small parties, they should probably be encouraged to consider merging with other parties to have more impact on our politics.

While most of these small parties will never be significant, in our environment where two out of the last Presidential elections have required a run-off, they will continue to be relevant. Also, during

Parliamentary elections, these parties, together with independents, affect the outcome by siphoning votes from one side or the other.

On their own, the small parties must consider whether their focus on Presidential elections is the best or they will be better off focusing just on parliamentary seats and alliances at the Presidential level.

To be fair, while the mechanics for including them in debates is difficult to work out, the inclusion of the small parties in debates will increase their support and make them more appealing. In the US Presidential elections in 1992, Ross Perot was included in the debates and ended up with almost 20% of the votes. Four years later, when he was excluded from the debates, his support was far less.

The introduction of public funding for political parties will strengthen the small parties that qualify significantly.

One of the major strategic blunders by the NPP was not forming alliances with the smaller parties over Parliamentary seats. If that had been done, the Sissala seats, seats in Bolga, Dr Nduom's old seat, and a few in the Northern and Volta region's would have gone to parties other than the NDC and denied them the numbers in the first round which gave them the propaganda advantage in the second round. Also, during the second, round, the resultant goodwill would have been very beneficial to the NPP.

CHAPTER FIFTEEN
THE AFTERMATH OF DEFEAT

THE DAY AFTER THE EC CHAIR declared Professor Mills the President-elect, a meeting was convened to discuss the situation.

At the meeting, it was decided that the candidate should address the media on the declaration.

During the meeting, Nana Akufo-Addo revealed that he had been approached by some clerics, at the request of Professor Mills to arrange a meeting between the two of them. While during the negotiations he had been made to understand that this would be a meeting without pre-conditions, when he got to the venue, things changed. With both of them at the site but in different rooms, Prof. Mills sent word that Nana Akufo-Addo should concede as a condition for the meeting. He declined to do so and the meeting was called off.

When we turned our attention to the text of Nana Akufo-Addo's expected statement, there was a very strong sentiment that legal avenues should be pursued vigorously. It was felt by most people that we had a very strong legal basis for contesting the results.

When the statement was read, the carefully nuanced avoidance of the word "concession" was completely lost on the media and the public. They read the congratulation of Professor Mills as an implied concession.

As the reality started hitting home that we had lost power, people started looking for scapegoats. There were rumours of sabotage and misapplication of funds. Supporters who had only a few weeks ago idolized some party and campaign leaders turned on them. In many cases, the same amount of money was said to have been misappropriated at three levels, the national, regional and constituency levels.

THANKSGIVING SERVICE

As party faithful demanded that something should be done, a thanksgiving service was organized at the Trade Fair Site on 11th of January, 2009. It was very popular and soon similar visits to thank Ghanaians and supporters were scheduled for many of the major towns and cities.

CHAPTER SIXTEEN
WHY AND HOW THE NPP LOST

"Opposition parties do not win elections, incumbent parties lose power"

Anonymous

ELECTION DAY

THE STORY OF HOW WE LOST this elections should begin on election day.

On election-day, more than 50% of Ghanaians woke up intending to vote for the NPP. Indeed, at the beginning of 2007, about 55% of Ghanaians would have voted for the NPP in a Presidential election and given us a healthy Parliamentary majority. This book has been mainly about how we got from that level to election-day where we had a bare, but firm majority. This chapter is about how we failed to translate that into votes.

First, let me remind you of the Press Conference that was addressed by Dr. Kofi Konadu Apraku, the NPP Campaign Director, a few days before the elections. In that Press Conference, he charged that people infiltrated by the NPP into the NDC had revealed that there was a plan to increase spoiled ballots in NPP strongholds by putting indelible ink marks on ballots in NPP strongholds.

Well, Dr. Apraku was right. After the first round, it was revealed, after the second round had been announced that 205, 438 ballots were rejected, mostly in NPP strongholds. It means that without these high levels of rejection, Nana Akufo-Addo would probably have been the one-touch winner of the 2008 election. For a real example of the effect of spoilt ballots, let us look at Ellembelle constituency.

In Mr Blay's loss, 5,590 out of the total of 35,302 ballots cast were spoiled. That is 15.8% of the ballots. These were probably not just routinely spoiled ballots. There appeared to have been an orchestrated campaign to defeat Mr. Blay. If it was done there, was it done elsewhere?

Second, let us look at Ablekuma South, where in the same election, after leading convincingly in the early hours of the night, Mr. Kojo Smith managed to lose by 5000 while Nana Addo was winning by 5000. In the end, when Mr Smith decided to protest, it turned out that he had barely 86 of the 140 polling station results he needed. As Mac Manu put it "there goes another seat".

Third, let us look at Asutifi South, where Collins Dauda won by just 14 votes. While it appeared that the court found that he had been duly elected, nothing like that actually happened. The court only said that the EC was freed from the injunction against declaring the results. In other words, the court never looked into whether or not ballot papers from Tikobo number two and number one were swapped on the way to the collation center or not. In other words, if those ballots were swapped, why were they swapped and what else happened while they were being swapped? Were some votes added? Were some taken out?

Fourth, how come that when Sheik I.C. Quaye and Shirley Ayorkor Botcway demanded recounts, their votes and/or that of their Presidential candidates increased significantly? If those errors could happen in Accra, where else did they happen?

Fifth, there is Volta Region in the second round that has already been discussed.

These are the reasons that many believe that we had more support on Election Day but we were beaten by a superior "ways and means" operation on voting day.

POLLS

Another thing that bolsters those claiming that some unusual things happened on Election Day were the polls. With the exception of one spurious poll that was instantly discredited by most experts, all the pre-election polls had the NPP ahead by 8 to 10 points. In other words, the question really was not whether the NPP would win or not, it was whether we could win one-touch or not.

ELECTION MONITORS

Many who disagree that rigging occurred cite the reports of foreign Election Monitors to support claims that the Elections were fair. There were less than 2000 Election Monitors and 22000 polling stations. How many of these stations spread across the country could they really monitor?

Nana with EU Monitoring team

PREPARATIONS FOR ELECTION DAY

Earlier in this book, I have recounted the problems with the selection of Returning Officers, polling agents and with getting our supporters to the polling stations. All these played their part in the final results.

CONTRIBUTARY FACTORS

First, the global economic environment made things difficult for incumbents. The increases in the price of fuel and food in 2007 and 2008 increased the cost of living generally. This fuelled the perception that there was "no money in our pockets".

GOVERNMENT LAPSES

Second, our government was not sensitive enough to the "NECCESSITIES" of the election-year politics. There were problems which were not tackled and initiatives that should not have been taken.

While it may be impolitic to say so, there are good policies that do not make good politics at particular times. It is reported that in early 1933, a distinguished group of economists made some recommendations to President Roosevelt. After listening to what they had to say, the President said "You guys know more about economics than I will ever know but I know more about politics than you will ever know. What you are recommending may be sound economics but it is not sound politics. Therefore, I will not do it."

We failed to reduce adequately and in a timely manner the price of fuel which would have helped many Ghanaians. Also in this category was the failure to deal with the controversy surrounding pre-mix fuel in the fishing communities along our coast. In Kumasi and Accra, city officials expelled traders from market-stalls and streets malls without any alternative arrangements in place and thus cost us crucial support amongst these groups. Also alienated were commercial drivers who were given draconian fines for trivial offenses.

On the other hand, the construction of the Jubilee House and the purchase of Presidential jets in an election year portrayed the NPP and the Kufuor administration as pre-occupied with priorities not important to ordinary people.

This gave credence to opposition charges that the NPP was an uncaring government.

Then we compounded it all by forcing eight of our best Ministers to resign because they were running for President and then sacking our National Security Co-ordinator/Minster, Francis Poku in an election year! Many believed that the Security problems we had in the period leading to and during the elections would have been better handled by a team led by Francis Poku. This is not to criticize Dr. Amo Ghartey. He is an excellent professional but many feel he needed a bit of time in the saddle before facing the challenges of election-year.

Of our government's failures, perhaps the most significant were the failure to provide adequate security, to our own polling station agents in the Volta Region and elsewhere and by implication, the Electoral Commission.

PARTY LAPSES

Third, our party, despite its glorious past, was a pale shadow of itself. It lacked, on the ground, the vital structures that in the past had brought us victory. Polling station executives had ceased to function; constituency executives were more interested in chasing money than chasing votes and campaign had been reduced, for most people into celebrity events in which one went to be seen rather than to campaign for votes. The end result was that while the NDC were going door-to-door, we were deriding them instead of going person-to-person ourselves.

Fourth, our campaign made too many mistakes.

People spent too much time putting one another down instead of working to defeat the NDC.

People with critical information were excluded or not consulted about things where their knowledge was crucial to success. Examples of these have been given in the course of this book.

There was too much emphasis on the candidate with the result that all of us wanted to follow him regardless of where we were truly needed. The result was that our candidate was overworked while others just looked on. While the NDC had three teams in the field, despite having enough talent to field six, we had one for most of the campaign and finally two for the last month or so.

We did not use our candidate's time well. Due to poor planning, our candidate spent too much time in certain regions where not much could be gained and too little time in places where his presence could have made a difference. For example, if the NPP candidate had spent more time in the eastern region or Greater Accra instead of the Volta Region, it would have made a decisive difference. In Eastern region, the candidate's home region, he underperformed President Kufuor by a whopping 64 thousand votes in the December 7th poll.

In communication, the NDC made propaganda a key part of their campaign while we talked, but never committed the necessary resources to counter their propaganda. Week after week, we agreed to commit more resources but did not.

USING PRESIDENT KUFUOR

This point has already been made but it bears emphasizing. As late as September of 2008, President Kufuor was more popular than either candidate running and yet, he did not get involved in the public phase of the campaign. There is no doubt that having the President on the campaign trail from September onwards in Central, Ashanti, Brong-Ahafo and Western Region would have made a significant difference. This was rather reminiscent of the 2000 US elections when the failure to get President Clinton involved had cost Democratic candidate Al Gore Arkansas and with that the Presidency.

RELATIONSHIP WITH SMALLER PARTIES

Also, our failure to nurture our relationship with the smaller parties over the last eight years also came to bear in that over the preceding eight years, these parties had moved, almost imperceptibly, from being our natural allies to being our natural opponents. Therefore, most of them, with the exception of the DFP, worked to help the NDC.

SUPPORT OF CORE CONSTITUENCIES

We lost the support of teachers and security personnel.

While their numbers in electoral terms are not significant, these two groups are crucial to electoral success. Most of the Electoral Commissions temporary Election workers are teachers and as we approached the elections, a lot of teachers were unhappy with arrears and being made to forfeit pay for going on strike. As one teacher who was an election official remarked afterwards, "we taught the NPP a lesson". In the NDC strategic document prepared in 2006, they made reaching out to security forces a key task. There is speculation that the reluctance of security forces to secure the vote in the Volta region and to secure the environment in Tain for a fair vote may have reflected the NDC's success in wooing them.

NDC CAMPAIGN

While it is true that the NPP lost this election, the NDC, apart from election-day ways and means, at which they excelled, did other things well too.

They had a clear strategy on how to deploy their big guns and they followed it well.

They had a clear propaganda strategy and they followed it and put resources behind it.

They exploited our government's election-year blunders ruthlessly, and in the process, lied recklessly wherever it served their interests.

PERSONAL MISTAKES

Many have asked whether there are things I would do differently and the answer is yes.

First, I assumed wrongly that given the importance of communications, enough resources and attention would be allocated to it. I was wrong. I should have been more aggressive in fighting for resources and space for my committee. I should have disregarded the campaigns injunctions not to seek outside help for my committee sooner.

Second, I was urged repeatedly to spend more time following the candidate. I was wrong in not heeding that advice. I realized during the second round that in the candidate's travelling entourage, my committee had not had a strong voice in the early parts of the campaign. Having the system we had in the second round, which involved having me on the road with the candidate and with daily conferences with Jake and Oboshie in Accra would have served the campaign very well.

CHAPTER SEVENTEEN
THE WAY FORWARD

" You are not going to be alone.
We will be with you in this fight for liberty.
And if our spirit is right, and our courage firm, the world will be with
us."

British Prime Minister, Tony Blair in 2001

"Not everything that is faced can be changed, but nothing can be
changed until it is faced."

James Baldwin

THE GLOBAL ENVIRONMENT

THE FACTORS THAT WILL DETERMINE THE outcome of the 2012 elections
are known but their significance is not yet clear.

The most significant factor will be the global environment. To the
extent that the global financial crisis improves, incumbent governments
will benefit. If in 2012, the world's economies have all turned round
and the cedi has picked up significantly against the dollar, the NDC
will benefit from that.

THE NDC PERFORMANCE

The second factor will be the performance and image of the NDC and President Mills. If by 2012, most Ghanaians see that they are better off than they are now and the NDC is clean, humble and united, it will help their chances of getting re-elected. On the other hand, if they are seen as unsuccessful, divided and arrogant, the NPP will benefit. Of course, as Churchill showed after the Second World War, and the U.S. Democrats showed in 2000 by losing, it is possible for good incumbents to lose power. Indeed, the NPP showed the same thing in 2008. Already, the NDC is breaking its election-year promises with reckless abandon.

LEADERSHIP OF NPP

The third factor will be the leadership of the NPP at all levels. This will be Constituency, Regional and National leaderships. If the NPP have energetic, united selfless and humble leadership, its chances will be significantly enhanced. Too often our leaders are interested in being rather than doing.

The fourth factor will be the process for choosing its leader. If the NPP process is seen as fair, dignified and not overtly influenced by money, the party will be united and the candidate will have enhanced credibility.

The fifth factor will be who the candidates are. There is quiet speculation about whether President Mills can and will run again. If he can run again, it will save the NDC from a potentially divisive primary contest. If he cannot ran again, the winner on the NDC side might emerge as the leader of a divided party and the NPP will benefit from this. On the NPP side, a nasty fight for the nomination characterized by personal attacks will leave whoever emerges as the nominee weakened and, therefore, more likely to lose the general elections to the NDC.

FLOATING VOTERS

The sixth factor will be the mood and inclinations of the floating voters.

For many years to come, no party can win elections without the floating voters. In addition, predictions about who might be President must of necessity start and end with the floating voters and regions. The youth, Central, Greater Accra and Western Regions will determine our Presidents for many years to come.

The seventh factor will be the messages and the messengers. Divisive messages and messengers do not attract floating voters and whoever grasps this and orients their message towards the future will win.

As U.S. President Bill Clinton used to say, "Elections are always about the future". Vitriolic attacks based on the past will not move floating voters to the polls or towards any candidate.

THE SMALL PARTIES

The eighth factor will be the small parties. Since there is always the possibility of a run-off, whoever the smaller parties are inclined to will start off with a significant advantage. In the two run-offs we have had since 1992, the candidate favoured by the small parties has won both times. Therefore, it stands to reason that the candidate or party favoured by these parties will probably win again.

RETURNING TO CORE PRINCIPLES

Ultimately, however, what ails the NPP is not a crisis about our constitution or about elections. It is crisis of spirit. The party that had grown accustomed to pulling itself up by its bootstraps suddenly became dependent on government. That is why we went out like guardians of our nation and took power from the NDC in 2000 while we whined about why the government would not protect us in 2000.

We need to move away from judging people in our party based on what their fathers and grandfathers did and let everyone make their own way in their generation. We need to move away from our over-reliance on age because the face of our country is young and the faces of our party must match that.

The fact of the matter is that if we put our house in order, pick good parliamentary candidates, get our people to vote, get our votes counted such that we have each and everyone of the 22 thousand polling station results signed and verified on election day of 2012, nobody can steal it from us.

To our leaders, let me end with some history.

In 1856, Abraham Lincoln wanted to be a Republican Senator. He had 52 of the 60 votes he needed to win but his opponent would elect a Senator from the other party rather than Lincoln. Lincoln put his party ahead of his own ambition by helping to elect his opponent. In 1860, his time came and he won the Presidency. In 1939 in Britain, Lord Halifax was a legitimate contender for the Premiership when Chamberlain resigned after his "Peace in our time fiasco". But Lord Halifax did not have blind ambition and he loved his country. Therefore he stepped aside because "At this time in our history, Churchill will be a better Prime Minister." Let us have leaders who love our party more than themselves so that we can restore the NPP to its natural place, Parliamentary majority and the Presidency. Let our leaders think of the old man who danced so joyously when he believed we had won at campaign headquarters on December 7th and wept so bitterly when he learned we had lost. Let them think of the sacrifices of J.B. Danquah, Obetsebi-Lamptey, R.R. Amponsah and others and realize that it is not about them. It is about something larger than their narrow self interests.

UNITY

To win, unity will be crucial. Not just at the National level but at all levels.

With Unity and very minimal efforts, here are some new constituencies we will pick:

Abura-Asebu-Kwamankese, Cape Coast, Salaga, Yendi, Yagaba-Kabore, Ablekuma-South, Winneba, Asutifi-South, Komenda-Edina-Eguafo-Ebirem. There are more.

As for coming back, it can be done.

We can do it.

So, let it be done, beginning right now.

Let us move forward, together.

Nana doing the "kangaroo dance" during the campaign.

INDEX